The Spokesman

Confessions of a Terrorist
Edited by Ken Coates
Published by Spokesman for the
Bertrand Russell Peace Foundation

Spokesman 78   2003

CONTENTS

Editorial 3

Confessions of a Terrorist 7   *John le Carré*

Word from Porto Alegre
Call of the 12
World Social Movements

Creating a Different World 16   *Noam Chomsky*

Confronting Empire 28   *Arundhati Roy*

Full Spectrum Democracy 32   *Ken Coates*

Kurt Vonnegut *versus* 37
the !&#*!@

Written in the Night 41   *John Berger*

Word from Cordoba
Pax Americana 46   *Edy Korthals Altes*
Fata Morgana!

'War on Terrorism' – 52   *Bahey el din Hassan*
War against Human Rights

Why Chernobyl Still Matters 56   *Rosalie Bertell*

Peace Dossier 71   *Iraq's Censored Declaration*
Torture on Diego Garcia?
Spying on the UN
'Shock and Awe' War
Against Pre-emption

Reviews 86   *Graham Macklin*
Michael Barratt Brown
Tony Simpson

Printed by the Russell Press Ltd., Nottingham, UK
ISSN 0262 7922   ISBN 0 85124 678 8

Subscriptions
Institutions £30.00
Individuals £20.00 (UK)
£25.00 (ex UK)
€40/$40

Back issues available on request

A CIP catalogue record for this book is available from the British Library

Published by the
Bertrand Russell Peace Foundation Ltd.,
Russell House
Bulwell Lane
Nottingham NG6 0BT
England
Tel. 0115 9784504
email:
elfeuro@compuserve.com
www.spokesmanbooks.com
www.russfound.org

Editorial Board:
Michael Barratt Brown
Ken Coates
John Daniels
Ken Fleet
Stuart Holland
Tony Simpson

Support the coalition for peace

Stop the War

BILL MORRIS
General Secretary

TONY WOODLEY
Deputy General Secretary

tel: 020 7611 2500

fax: 020 7611 2555

For further information visit our website
www.tgwu.org.uk

Transport and General Workers' Union

Editorial
Europe against the War?

On Tuesday March 4th, the British Foreign Secretary threatened not Saddam Hussein, but his opposite numbers in France and Germany with condign punishment if they failed to support the so-called 'second' resolution in the Security Council of the United Nations, paving the way for the Anglo-American attack on Iraq. Mr. Straw insisted that at stake was the commitment of the United States to multilateral initiatives and organisations such as the United Nations itself and Nato. If Europe refuses to fall into line, he said, dire consequences will follow:

> '… you are right it is the United States which has the military power to act as the world's policeman, and only the United States. We live in a uni-polar world; the United States has a quarter of the world's wealth, the world's GDP, and it has stronger armed forces than the next 27 countries put together. So its predominance is huge. That is a fact. No one can gainsay it; no one can change it in the short or medium term. The choice we have to make in the international community is whether, in a uni-polar world, we want the only super-power to act unilaterally and we force them to act unilaterally or whether we work in such a way that they act within the multilateral institutions. What I say to France and Germany and all my other European Union colleagues is to take care, because just as America helps to define and influence our politics, so what we do in Europe helps to define and influence American politics. We will reap a whirlwind if we push the Americans into a unilateralist position in which they are the centre of this uni-polar world.'

This inelegant and sycophantic argument well suits the British Foreign Secretary, who has not frequently distinguished himself by any claims to independence of judgement. Quite naturally he deems it wrong to argue with anyone so rich, leave alone so powerful, as the keeper of the whirlwind.

No sooner had he completed his statement to the House of Commons Foreign Affairs Select Committee than the Foreign Secretary was embracing Russian Foreign Minister Ivanov, and receiving his blunt message that Russia would not abstain in the vote on the proposed war resolution in the Security Council but would, if necessary, oppose it to prevent a war. Politely, Mr. Straw did him the courtesy of disbelieving him, a favour which is normally accorded to Mr. Straw himself by the British people. Towards the similar statement by M. Chirac, a more ambivalent disbelief has been expressed. Part of the British establishment says he will, and the rest assume won't, veto.

These questions will all be resolved by the time these words appear in print. It is not excluded that some surprises may be in store for us. But what is abundantly plain is that the British Government has not found it easy to recruit support for its project for a second resolution and indeed has needed to make continuous efforts to retain the support of Bulgaria and Spain for its original proposal. As it seeks to develop alternative proposals which might appeal to the six independent non-permanent members of the Security Council, it is by no means excluded that it will lose the support of the United States. Possibly the doubts expressed by Donald Rumsfeld, as to whether Britain would or would not be participating in the early phase of the coming war were a not very coded message that Britain must hurry up with the diplomacy so that he can get on with the war.

The Foreign Secretary is right: this is a phenomenal development. Here we have the United States, as the Foreign Secretary insists, the foremost military power in the world, with a war machine which dwarfs all others combined, and an economy of unparalleled puissance, manifestly unable to prevail, not only over the old Europeans, but also even over small African countries or its Latin American neighbours. Worse, in a related sphere, the great United States has been frustrated by the resurgent democracy of Turkey, whose Parliament has blocked the deployment of a massive United States army, designed for the conquest of Northern Iraq. No doubt Jack Straw will be fulminating also against the Turks and summoning up his borrowed whirlwinds to compass their destruction. Are these all idle threats? It is to be feared that they are not: but it is also clear that threats will not be enough to stem the global upsurge which Straw is confronting. Behind the welcome diplomatic obduracy stands the million-headed democracy of a world which is refusing war.

We have repeatedly drawn attention to the sinister development of military doctrine in the United States, which specifically celebrates the idea of Full Spectrum Dominance on land, sea, air and space, not to say information. The machines have been perfected to enforce such domination, but there is a snag in the game plan: people cannot be persuaded that the new dominion will be just, or even tolerable.

Straw may be right that the whirlwind of American wrath may blow away all such scruples. But perhaps there remains some hope that democracy, having reasserted itself in all those vast mass demonstrations, not only in Turkey and old Europe, but also in the United States itself, might quickly reach out to defend its scope and reach, and prevent the destruction of its values during the onslaught of brute Full Spectrum Dominance.

Evidently the present conflict has divided the whole world. The United States has many residual allies, and not all of them by any means have been bought or blackmailed. In Eastern Europe, there are American allies with ideals. Even so, a very large majority of the peoples of East European countries are expressing themselves against war. Spain and Italy seethe with rejection of their Governments' alignments, and it appears doubtful whether these commitments can be maintained. Whirlwinds may well be lurking, but Jack Straw needs better forecasting technology if he is going to predict where they will strike, and who they will undermine. At this moment, it seems possible that they will visit London.

The fact remains that the world does need acceptable alternatives to Full Spectrum Dominance. The beginning of wisdom is to understand who is intended to be dominated. Clearly it is not enemies who should fear this potent influence. They will be dealt with at the convenience of the dominator, but they constitute the least of his problems.

What this crisis has made abundantly plain is what we have been saying for some considerable time: that the principal targets of this military doctrine are the allies, who are the ones who must fear whirlwinds if they displease the hegemon. But there is another candidate for domination, perhaps even more seriously at risk than the allies: and this is the American people themselves, who are supposed, uncomplainingly, to sustain and pay for all this massive structure of intimidation and terror, and to suffer the global loathing which it engenders.

What today shows is that it is time for all these worms to turn. Europe can do much to encourage this process, because it already has devised a confederal means of association, very much rooted in the pacifism which gripped the French and German populations at the end of the Second World War. This pacifism has not exhausted itself, and can play an honourable part in the recovery of Europe's dynamism, based, not on domination, but on democratic association. Is it not time to consider again how exactly Russia should be invited to relate to this truly European process, and what protections and safeguards it may need to play its full part in a new architecture of co-operation?

The most hopeful prospect for Europe emerges from the growing identity between France, Germany and Russia. No doubt Jack Straw is right, to say that whirlwinds may attend each of these countries if they stand separately. The pressures on President Chirac are already phenomenal, and the propaganda machine of Britain and the United States is not yet fully cranked up to Full Spectrum Dominance of information. Nonetheless, even at half cock, the capacity for spin and outright lies is not small, and it is but a foretaste of what should be expected after the war.

The war will be illicit, since it is not possible to obtain the sanction of the Security Council, and by no stretch of the imagination can it be presented as a matter of self-defence. British soldiers will be under especial pressure, because Britain, unlike the United States, has recognised the authority of the International Criminal Court, which does not accept the age-old alibi that armed forces may avoid prosecution by pleading obedience to orders. Life for the British Government is therefore likely to become extremely complex and difficult. But for Russia, Germany and France, whilst there will remain many problems, there are clear advantages in continuing and deepening their co-operation. Together, they are far from frail.

Today we are in a reverse position from that which pertained at the end of the Cold War. The Russian military was a formidable force, and in some respects it was technologically more advanced than its American adversary. It crashed, not in a military contest, but because its economic underpinning could no longer sustain it. Unheard of investment was pre-empted by the military-industrial complex, and the Americans, quite literally, outspent their opponents to the point of collapse. Now, the most awesome military machine is being cranked up by the

United States, and the embodiment of Full Spectrum Dominance flexes its muscles.

But the weakness of purely military power has never been more clear. The popular upheaval against this war has not taken place in solidarity with Saddam Hussein. There is an overwhelming sympathy with the Iraqi population, half of whom are children, who face the most brutal bombardment. But far more than this, there is a dawning appreciation of the impossibility of accepting world government by a militaristic power, drawing its sole legitimacy from the power of the gun. Jack Straw's warnings all have the opposite effect to that intended.

The emergence of a new European identity can prefigure a new European unity, based not on armed force, but on solid economic co-operation, and social advance. The whole world wants better possibilities of development, improved schools, health, and pensions, not space lasers which can vaporise whole communities at the touch of a button on the other side of the globe.

The arguments which divide the European States will necessarily continue until they are resolved: but resolving them requires a profound revaluation of European ideals and objectives, and the renovation of European institutions. All this will be of clear interest to the new Turkish democracy, if it is not snuffed out in the gathering hysteria of war.

The necessary revaluation may not take place quickly, or even in time. If it does not, then the persistence of the problem of military imbalance and economic inequality will continue to ensure its necessity. But another world is possible: among all the threats of high level bombardment, mass murder, and unconscionable destruction, and among any moral whirlwinds which may be offered to carry off the French and German Governments, but are far more likely to carry off the British, there is, is there not, a moment of opportunity, in which we could refashion the framework of our international associations, and rediscover the lineaments of convergence for peace?

Ken Coates

Confessions of a Terrorist

John le Carré

John le Carré raised the spy thriller to a high art form. His The Spy Who Came in from the Cold *won him a global reputation. As the Cold War recedes into history, his talents are finding renewed expression in portraying the tortured condition of the new world order.*

America has entered one of its periods of historical madness, but this is the worst I can remember: worse than McCarthyism, worse than the Bay of Pigs and in the long term potentially more disastrous than the Vietnam war.

The reaction to 9/11 is beyond anything Osama could have hoped for in his nastiest dreams. As in McCarthy times, the domestic rights and freedoms that have made America the envy of the world are being systematically eroded.

The hounding of non-national US residents continues apace. 'Non-permanent' males of North Korean and Middle Eastern descent are disappearing into secret imprisonment on secret charges on the secret word of judges. US-resident Palestinians who were formerly ruled stateless, and therefore not deportable, are being handed over to Israel for 'resettlement' in Gaza and the West Bank, places where they may never have set foot before.

Are we playing the same game here in Britain? I expect so. Another thirty years and we'll be allowed to know.

The combination of compliant US media and vested corporate interests is once more ensuring that a debate that should be ringing out in every town square is confined to the loftier columns of the East Coast press: see page A27 if you can find and understand it.

No American administration has ever held its cards so close to its chest. If the intelligence services know nothing, that will be the best-kept secret of all. Remember that these are the same organisations who brought us the biggest failure in intelligence history: 9/11.

The imminent war was planned years before Osama bin Laden struck, but it was Osama who made it possible. Without Osama, the Bush junta would still be trying to explain such tricky matters as how it came to be elected in the first place; Enron; its shameless favouring of the already-too-rich; its reckless disregard for the world's poor, the ecology and a raft of unilaterally abrogated international treaties. They might also have to be telling us why they support Israel in its continuing disregard for UN resolutions.

But Osama conveniently swept all that under the carpet. The US defence budget has been raised by another $60 billion to around $360 billion. A splendid new generation of US nuclear weapons is in the pipeline, tailored to respond equally to nuclear, chemical and biological weapons in the hands of 'rogue states'. So we can all breathe easy.

And America is not only deciding unilaterally who may or may not possess these weapons. It also reserves to itself the unilateral right to deploy its own nuclear weapons without compunction whenever and wherever it considers its interests, friends and allies threatened. Precisely who these friends and allies are going to be over the next years will, as ever in politics, be a bit of a conundrum. You make nice friends and allies, so you arm them to the teeth. Then one day they're not your friends and allies any more, so you nuke them.

It is worth remembering here for just how many long hours, and how deeply, the US cabinet weighed the option of nuking Afghanistan in the wake of 9/11. Happily for all of us, but for the Afghans in particular whose complicity in 9/11 was much less than Pakistan's, they decided to make do with 25,000 ton 'conventional' daisy-cutters, which by all accounts deliver as much clout as a small nuke anyway. But next time it'll be for real.

Quite what war Americans think they are supporting is a lot less clear. A war for how long, please? At what cost in American lives? At what cost to the American taxpayer's pocket? At what cost in Iraqi lives? It is probably by now a state secret, but Desert Storm cost Iraq at least twice as many lives as America lost in the entire Vietnam war.

How Bush and his junta succeeded in deflecting America's anger from Osama bin Laden to Saddam Hussein is one of the great public relations conjuring tricks of history. But they swung it.

The American public is not merely being misled. It is being threatened, bullied, browbeaten and kept in a permanent state of ignorance and fear, with a consequent dependence upon its leadership. The carefully orchestrated neurosis should, with any luck, carry Bush and his fellow conspirators nicely into the next election.

Those who are not with Mr. Bush are against him. Worse – see his speech of January 3rd – they are with the enemy. Which is odd, because I'm dead against Bush, but I would love to see Saddam's downfall – just not on Bush's terms and not by his methods. And not under the banner of such outrageous hypocrisy.

Old-style American colonialism is about to spread its iron wings over all of us. More Quiet Americans are slipping into unsuspecting townships than at the height of the Cold War.

The religious cant that will send American troops into battle is perhaps the most sickening aspect of this surreal war-to-be. Bush has an arm-lock on God.

And God has very particular political opinions.

God appointed America to save the world in any way that suits America.

God appointed Israel to be the nexus of America's Middle Eastern policy, and anyone who wants to mess with that idea is: (a) anti-Semitic, (b) anti-American, (c) with the enemy, and (d) a terrorist.

God also has pretty scary connections. In America, where all men are equal in His sight, if not in one another's, the Bush family numbers one President, one ex-President, one ex-head of the CIA, the governor of Florida and the ex-governor of Texas. Bush Senior has some good wars to his credit, and a well-earned reputation for visiting America's wrath on disobedient client states. One little war he hand-launched was against his own former CIA pal, Manuel Noriega of Panama, who served him well in the Cold War but got too big for his boots when it was over. Power doesn't come much more naked than that, and Americans know it.

Care for a few pointers?

George W. Bush. 1978-84: senior executive, Arbusto Energy/Bush Exploration, an oil company. 1986-1990: on the board of the Harken oil company.

Dick Cheney. 1995-2000: chief executive of the Halliburton oil company.

Condoleezza Rice. 1991-2000: on the board of the Chevron oil company, which named an oil tanker after her.

And so on.

But none of these trifling associations affects the integrity of God's work. We're talking honest values here. And we know where your children go to school.

In 1993, while ex-President George Bush was paying a social visit to the ever-democratic Kingdom of Kuwait to receive their thanks for liberating them, somebody tried to kill him. The CIA believes that 'somebody' was Saddam Hussein. Hence Bush Junior's cry: 'That man tried to kill my Daddy.' But it's still not personal, this war. It's still necessary. It's still God's work. It's still about bringing freedom and democracy to the poor, oppressed Iraqi people.

To be an acceptable member of the Bush team it seems you must also believe in Absolute Good and Absolute Evil, and Bush, with a lot of help from his friends, family and God, is there to tell us which is which. I think I may be Evil for writing this, but I'll have to check.

What Bush won't tell us is the truth about why we're going to war. What is at stake is not an Axis of Evil – but oil, money and people's lives. Saddam's misfortune is to sit on the second biggest oilfield in the world. Iran's, next door, is to possess the world's largest repositories of natural gas. Bush wants both, and who helps him get them will receive a piece of the cake. And who doesn't, won't.

If Saddam didn't have the oil, he could torture and murder his citizens to his heart's content. Other leaders do it every day – think Saudi Arabia, think Pakistan, think Turkey, think Syria, think Egypt – but these are our friends and allies.

In reality, I suspect, Baghdad represents no clear and present danger to its neighbours, and none to America or Britain. Saddam's weapons of mass destruction, if he's still got them, will be peanuts by comparison with the stuff Israel or America could hurl at him at five minutes' notice. What is at stake is not an imminent military or terrorist threat, but the economic imperative of American growth.

What is at stake is America's need to demonstrate its over-arching military power to all of us – to Europe and Russia and China, and poor mad little North Korea, as well as the Middle East; to show who rules America at home, and who is to be ruled by America abroad.

The most charitable interpretation of Tony Blair's part in all this is that he believed that, by riding the tiger, he could steer it. He can't. Instead, he gave it a phoney legitimacy, and a smooth voice. Now I fear, the same tiger has him penned into a corner, and he can't get out. Ironically, George W. himself may be feeling a little bit the same way.

In One-Party Britain, Blair on a lousy turnout was elected supreme leader by about a quarter of the electorate. Given the same public apathy and the continued dismal showing by the opposition parties at the next election, Blair or his successor will achieve similar absolute power with an even smaller proportion of the vote. It is utterly laughable that, at a time when Blair has talked himself against the ropes, neither of Britain's opposition leaders can lay a glove on him. But that's Britain's tragedy, as it is America's: as our governments spin, lie and lose their credibility, and the supposed parliamentary alternatives to them merely jockey for their clothes, the electorate simply shrugs and looks the other way. Politicians can never believe how little they deceive us.

So the point in Britain is not which political Party will form a government after the looming shambles, but who will be in the driving seat.

Blair's best chance of personal survival must be that, at the eleventh hour, world protest and an improbably emboldened UN will force Bush to put his gun back in his holster unfired. But what happens when the world's greatest cowboy rides back into town without a tyrant's head to wave at the boys?

Blair's worst chance is that, with or without the United Nations, he will drag us into a war that, if the will to negotiate energetically had ever been there, could have been avoided; a war that has been no more democratically debated in Britain than it has in America or the UN. By doing so, Blair will have helped provoke unforeseeable retaliation, great domestic unrest, and regional chaos in the Middle East. He will have set back our relations with Europe and the Middle East for decades to come. Welcome to the party of the Ethical Foreign Policy.

There is a middle way, but it's a tough one: Bush dives in without UN approval and Blair stays on the bank. Goodbye to the Special Relationship.

The stink of religious self-righteousness in the American air recalls the British Empire at its worst. Lord Curzon's cloak sits poorly on the shoulders of Washington's fashionably conservative columnists. I cringe even more when I hear my Prime Minister lend his Head Prefect's sophistries to this patently colonialist adventure. His very real anxieties about Terror are shared by all sane men. What he can't explain is how he reconciles a global assault on Al Qaeda with a territorial assault on Iraq.

We are in this war, if it takes place, in order to secure the fig-leaf of our special relationship with America, to grab our share of the oil pot, and because, after all the public hand-holding in Washington and Camp David, Blair has to show up at the altar.

'But will we win, Daddy?'

'Of course, child. It will all be over while you're still in bed.'

'Why?'

'Because otherwise Mr. Bush's voters will get terribly impatient and may decide not to vote for him after all.'

'But will people be killed, Daddy?'

'Nobody you know, darling. Just foreign people.'

'Can I watch it on television?'

'Only if Mr. Bush says you can.'

'And afterwards, will everything be normal again? Nobody will do anything horrid any more?'

'Hush, child, and go to sleep.'

Last Friday an American friend of mine in California drove to his local supermarket with a sticker on his car saying 'Peace is also Patriotic'. It was gone by the time he'd finished his shopping.

© David Cornwell 2003.

This is an expanded version of a contribution to the openDemocracy global debate on the Iraq crisis published on www.openDemocracy.net

Call of the World Social Movements

**Porto Alegre, Brazil
January 2003**

The World Social Forum brings together social movements and non-governmental organisations from across the world. In January, it met for the third time in Latin America. Resisting the war on Iraq and other conflicts figured high on its agenda, as this statement from the Forum makes clear. We follow it with interventions made in Porto Alegre by Noam Chomsky, Arundhati Roy and Ken Coates.

We are meeting in Porto Alegre in the shadow of a global crisis. The belligerent intentions of the United States Government in its determination to launch a war on Iraq pose a grave threat to us all, and are a dramatic manifestation of the links between militarism and economic domination.

At the same time, neo-liberal globalisation itself is in crisis: the threat of a global recession is ever present; corporate corruption scandals are daily news, and expose the reality of capitalism.

Social and economic inequalities are growing, threatening the social structures of our societies and cultures, our rights and our lives.

Biodiversity, air, water, forest, soil and sea are treated like commodities and are for sale.

All this threatens our common future.

We oppose this!

For our common future
We are social movements that are fighting all around the world against neo-liberal globalisation, war, racism, castism, poverty, patriarchy and all the forms of economic, ethnic, social, political, cultural, sexual and gender discriminations and exclusions. We are all fighting for social justice, citizenship, participatory democracy, universal rights and for the right of peoples to decide their own future.

We stand for peace and international co-operation, for a sustainable society answering the needs of people for food, housing, health, education, information, water, energy, public transportation and human rights.

We are in solidarity with the women engaged against social and patriarchal violence. We support the struggle of the peasants, workers, popular urban movements and all those who are urgently threatened by being deprived of homes, jobs, land and their rights.

We have demonstrated in millions to say that another world is possible.

This has never been more true and more urgent.

No war!
The social movements are against militarisation, the increase of military bases and state repression that create countless refugees and the criminalisation of social movements and poor people.

We are against the war on Iraq, the attacks on the Palestinian, Chechen and Kurdish peoples, the wars on Afghanistan, Colombia, in Africa and the growing threat of war on Korea. We oppose the economic and political aggression against Venezuela and the political and economic blockade by the United States Government against Cuba, and elsewhere. We are against all kinds of military and economic actions designed to impose the neo-liberal model and undermine the sovereignty and peace of peoples around the world.

War has become a structural and permanent part of global domination, using military force to control people and strategic resources such as oil. The United States government and its allies are imposing war as a more and more common solution for resolving conflicts. We also denounce the deliberate attempts made by imperialists to increase religious, ethnic, racist, tribal and other tensions and strife all over the world in order to pursue their selfish interests.

The majority of public opinion around the world is opposed to the coming war on Iraq. We call on all social movements and progressive forces to support, participate in and organise world-wide protests on February 15th 2003. These protests are already planned and co-ordinated by all those who oppose the war in over 30 major cities around the world.

Derail the World Trade Organisation
The World Trade Organisation (WTO), the Free Trade Area of the Americas (FTAA), and a proliferation of regional and bilateral trade agreements such as the Africa Growth and Opportunity Act (AGOA) and the proposed Central America free trade agreements are used by multinational corporations to promote their interests, to dominate and control our economies, and to impose a development model which impoverishes our societies. In the name of trade liberalisation, every aspect of life and nature is for sale and people are denied their basic rights. Agri-multinationals are trying to impose genetically modified organisms (GMOs) world-wide; people suffering from HIV/AIDS and other pandemics in Africa and elsewhere are denied access to cheap generic drugs. In addition, countries of the South are trapped in a never-ending cycle of debt that forces them to open up their markets and export their wealth.

In the coming year our campaigns against the World Trade Organisation, the Free Trade Area of the Americas, and trade liberalisation will grow in size and scope.

We will campaign to stop and reverse the liberalisation of agriculture, water, energy, public services and investment, and to reassert peoples' sovereignty over their societies, their resources, their cultures and knowledge, and their economies.

We are in solidarity with the Mexican farmers who say *'el campo no aguanta mas'* ('the farmers are fed up') and in the spirit of their struggles we will mobilise locally, nationally and internationally to derail the World Trade Organisation and the Free Trade Area of the Americas. We support the world-wide movement to fight for food sovereignty and against the neo-liberal models of agriculture, food production and distribution. In particular, we will organise mass protests around the world during the 5th ministerial meeting of the World Trade Organisation in Cancun, Mexico, in September 2003, and during the ministerial meeting of the Free Trade Area of the Americas in Miami, United States of America, in October.

Cancel the debt
The full and unconditional cancellation of Third World debt constitutes a prerequisite condition in order to fulfil even the most basic human rights. We shall support any indebted country that would stop its external debt payment and would break its agreements with the International Monetary Fund, especially the Structural Adjustment Programmes. Centuries of exploitation of the Third World people, their resources and environment have given them the right to reparations. We ask 'who owes whom'? These issues will be raised in the major campaigns being held in 2003; G8 (Evian/June), World Trade Organisation (Cancun/September) and the International Monetary Fund and World Bank annual meeting (Washington/September).

Opposing the G8
We call on all the social movements and progressive forces to be part of the mobilisation to denounce the illegitimacy and also to reject the policies of the G8 that will be meeting in Evian, France, from 1-3 June 2003. This mobilisation will also be organised all around the world, with an international gathering at Evian that will include an alternative summit, alternative camp and a huge international demonstration.

Women: promoting equality
We are part of the actions promoted by women's movements on 8th March, International Women's Day, to fight against all forms of violence and patriarchy and for social and political equality.

In solidarity
We call for solidarity from all progressive social forces, movements and organisations across the world for those peoples such as the Palestinians, Venezuelans, Bolivians and others who are facing extreme crisis at this very moment in time.

Enhance our international network
Last year during the World Social Forum in Porto Alegre we adopted a declaration that defines our aims, our struggles and the ways we build our alliances (see *Spokesman 74*). The spirit of this text is still living and will inspire our coming mobilisations.

Since then, the world has been changing very quickly and we feel the need to take a new step in our decision-making processes, in our co-ordinations and alliances; the need to promote a broad, radical, democratic, plural, internationalist, feminist, non-discriminatory and anti-imperialist agenda.

We now want to build a framework articulating our analyses and commitments to our mobilisations. This requires the active participation of all the movements, keeping in mind that the social forums are independent from governments and political parties (as given in the World Social Forum Charter of Principles) and keeping a respect for their autonomy. This framework would be strengthened by all the different social actors contributing and sharing their experiences and concrete social practices. Further, this would be in accordance with the different forms of political expression and organisation of the social movements, and with regard to the diversity of ideologies and cultures.

We feel the need to constitute a network of movements that is responsive, flexible and sustainable; yet is also broad and transparent. Its responsibilities should be to enrich and feed the process, to promote its diversity and to assume the necessary degree of co-ordination. The aims of the network will be to enhance the engagement of movements around the world in a deeper political debate, to facilitate common action and to strengthen the initiative of concrete actors fighting for social interests. Its work should be both horizontal and effective.

To this end we propose to build a contact group as a resource and tool for our international mobilisations, including preparing meetings, promoting debate and democracy by promoting a web site and mailing lists. This contact group would be established for a period of between six and twelve months and it will draw on the past experience of the supporters of the network of social and popular movements that are based in Brazil.

This arrangement is transitional and to ensure continuity. The main task of this provisory group is to facilitate debate so that the social movements around the world define concrete procedures to work together. It is an ongoing process. A first review of the new contact group will take place at meetings of the network of social movements during the mass mobilisation against the World Trade Organisation in Cancun in September 2003. A second review, again in assemblies of the network of social movements, will follow during the World Social Forum meeting that is expected to be held in India in 2004.

Among other things, the reviews will consider the effectiveness of the co-ordination and seek new ways to enhance it. It will also consider how to proceed from one year to the next, and how to include national, regional movements and thematic campaigns. In the meantime, we need a large debate among organisations, campaigns and networks to articulate the proposals for a more permanent and representative structure.

In the months to come we will have many occasions to experiment, improve and build this process through our campaigns and mobilisations.

We call for all networks, popular and social movements to sign this statement and send your signatures to movsoc@uol.com.br

Creating a Different World

Noam Chomsky

Noam Chomsky is Professor of Linguistics at the Massachusetts Institute of Technology. He spoke at the World Social Forum in Porto Alegre in Brazil on 27 January 2003.

We are meeting at a moment of world history that is in many ways unique – a moment that is ominous, but also full of hope.

The most powerful state in history has proclaimed, loud and clear, that it intends to rule the world by force, the dimension in which it reigns supreme. Apart from the conventional bow to noble intentions that is the standard (hence meaningless) accompaniment of coercion, its leaders are committed to pursuit of their 'imperial ambition,' as it is frankly described in the leading journal of the foreign policy establishment – critically, an important matter. They have also declared that they will tolerate no competitors, now or in the future. They evidently believe that the means of violence in their hands are so extraordinary that they can dismiss with contempt anyone who stands in their way. There is good reason to believe that the war with Iraq is intended, in part, to teach the world some lessons about what lies ahead when the empire decides to strike a blow – though 'war' is hardly the proper term, given the array of forces.

The doctrine is not entirely new, nor unique to the United States, but it has never before been proclaimed with such brazen arrogance – at least not by anyone we would care to remember.

I am not going to try to answer the question posed for this meeting: How to confront the empire? The reason is that most of you know the answers as well or better than I do, through your own lives and work. The way to 'confront the empire' is to create a different world, one that is not based on violence and subjugation, hate and fear. That is why we are here, and the World Social Forum offers hope that these are not idle dreams.

Yesterday I had the rare privilege of seeing some very inspiring work to achieve these goals, at the international gathering of the *Via Campesina* at a community of the Landless Workers' Movement (*Movimento dos*

Trabalhadores Rurais Sem Terra or MST), which I think is the most important and exciting popular movement in the world. With constructive local actions such as those of the Landless Workers' Movement, and international organisation of the kind illustrated by the *Via Campesina* and the World Social Forum, with sympathy and solidarity and mutual aid, there is real hope for a decent future.

I have also had some other recent experiences that give a vivid picture of what the world may be like if imperial violence is not limited and dismantled. Last month I was in south-eastern Turkey, the scene of some of the worst atrocities of the grisly 1990s, still continuing: just a few hours ago we were informed of renewed atrocities by the army near Diyarbakir, the unofficial capital of the Kurdish regions. Through the 1990s, millions of people were driven out of the devastated countryside, with tens of thousands killed and every imaginable form of barbaric torture. They try to survive in caves outside the walls of Diyarbakir, in condemned buildings in miserable slums in Istanbul, or wherever they can find refuge, barred from returning to their villages despite new legislation that theoretically permits return. 80% of the weapons came from the United States. In the year 1997 alone, Clinton sent more arms to Turkey than in the entire Cold War period combined, up to the onset of the state terror campaign – called 'counter-terror' by the perpetrators and their supporters, another convention. Turkey became the leading recipient of United States arms as atrocities peaked (apart from Israel-Egypt, a separate category).

In 1999, Turkey relinquished this position to Colombia. The reason is that in Turkey, the United States-backed state terror had largely succeeded, while in Colombia it had not. Colombia had the worst human rights record in the Western hemisphere in the 1990s and was by far the leading recipient of United States arms and military training, and now leads the world. It also leads the world by other measures, for example, murder of labour activists: more than half of those killed worldwide in the last decade were in Colombia. Close to half a million people were driven from their land last year, a new record. The displaced population is now estimated at 2.7 million. Political killings have risen to 20 a day; 5 years ago it was half that.

I visited Cauca in southern Colombia, which had the worst human rights record in the country in 2001, quite an achievement. There I listened to hours of testimony by peasants who were driven from their lands by chemical warfare – called 'fumigation' under the pretext of a United States-run 'drug war' that few take seriously and that would be obscene if that were the intent. Their lives and lands are destroyed, children are dying, they suffer from sickness and wounds. Peasant agriculture is based on a rich tradition of knowledge and experience gained over many centuries, in much of the world passed on from mother to daughter. Though a remarkable human achievement, it is very fragile, and can be destroyed forever in a single generation. Also being destroyed is some of the richest biodiversity in the world, similar to neighbouring regions of Brazil. *Campesinos*, indigenous people, Afro-Colombians can join the millions in rotting slums and camps. With the people gone, multinationals can come in to strip the mountains for coal and to extract oil and other resources, and to convert what is left of the land to mono-crop agri-export using laboratory-produced seeds in an environment shorn of its treasures and variety.

The scenes in Cauca and South-eastern Turkey are very different from the celebrations of the *Via Campesina* gathering at the Landless Workers' Movement community. But Turkey and Colombia are inspiring and hopeful in different ways, because of the courage and dedication of people struggling for justice and freedom, confronting the empire where it is killing and destroying. These are some of the signs of the future if 'imperial ambition' proceeds on its normal course, now to be accelerated by the grand strategy of global rule by force. None of this is inevitable, and among the good models for ending these crimes are the ones I mentioned: the Landless Workers' Movement, the *Via Campesina*, and the World Social Forum.

At the World Social Forum, the range of issues and problems under intense discussion is very broad, remarkably so, but I think we can identify two main themes. One is global justice and life after capitalism – or to put it more simply, life, because it is not so clear that the human species can survive very long under existing state capitalist institutions. The second theme is related: war and peace, and more specifically, the war in Iraq that Washington and London are desperately seeking to carry out, virtually alone.

Let's start with some good news about these basic themes. As you know, there is also a conference of the World Economic Forum going on right now, in Davos. Here in Porto Alegre, the mood is hopeful, vigorous, exciting. In Davos, the *New York Times* tells us, 'the mood has darkened.' For the 'movers and shakers,' it is not 'global party time' any more. In fact, the founder of the Forum has conceded defeat: 'The power of corporations has completely disappeared,' he said. So we have won. There is nothing left for us to do but pick up the pieces – not only to talk about a vision of the future that is just and humane, but to move on to create it.

Of course, we should not let the praise go to our heads. There are still a few difficulties ahead. The main theme of the World Economic Forum is 'Building Trust.' There is a reason for that. The 'masters of the universe,' as they liked to call themselves in more exuberant days, know that they are in serious trouble. They recently released a poll showing that trust in leaders has severely declined. Only the leaders of non-governmental organisations had the trust of a clear majority, followed by United Nations and spiritual/religious leaders, then leaders of Western Europe and economic managers, below them corporate executives, and well below them, at the bottom, leaders of the United States, with about 25% trust. That may well mean virtually no trust: when people are asked whether they trust leaders with power, they usually say 'Yes,' out of habit.

It gets worse. A few days ago a poll in Canada found that over one-third of the population regard the United States as the greatest threat to world peace. The United States ranks more than twice as high as Iraq or North Korea, and far higher than Al Qaeda as well. A poll without careful controls, by *Time* magazine, found that over 80% of respondents in Europe regarded the United States as the greatest threat to world peace, compared with less than 10% for Iraq or North Korea. Even if these numbers are wrong by some substantial factor, they are dramatic. Without going on, the corporate leaders who paid $30,000 to attend the sombre meetings in Davos have good reasons to take as their theme: 'Building Trust.'

The coming war with Iraq is undoubtedly contributing to these interesting and important developments. Opposition to the war is completely without historical precedent. In Europe it is so high that Secretary of 'Defence' Donald Rumsfeld dismissed Germany and France as just the 'old Europe,' plainly of no concern because of their disobedience. The 'vast numbers of other countries in Europe [are] with the United States,' he assured foreign journalists. These vast numbers are the 'new Europe,' symbolised by Italy's Berlusconi, soon to visit the White House, praying that he will be invited to be the third of the 'three B's': Bush-Blair-Berlusconi – assuming that he can stay out of jail. Italy is on board, the White House tells us. It is apparently not a problem that over 80% of the public is opposed to the war, according to recent polls. That just shows that the people of Italy also belong to the 'old Europe,' and can be sent to the ashcan of history along with France and Germany, and others who do not know their place.

Spain is hailed as another prominent member of the new Europe – with 75% totally opposed to the war, according to an international Gallup poll. According to the leading foreign policy analyst of *Newsweek*, pretty much the same is true of the most hopeful part of the new Europe, the former Communist countries that are counted on (quite openly) to serve United States interests and undermine Europe's despised social market and welfare states. He reports that in the Czeck Republic, two-thirds of the population oppose participation in a war, while in Poland only one-quarter would support a war even if the United Nations inspectors 'prove that Iraq possesses weapons of mass destruction.' The Polish press reports 37% approval in this case, still extremely low, at the heart of the 'new Europe.'

New Europe soon identified itself in an open letter in the *Wall Street Journal*: along with Italy, Spain, Poland and the Czeck Republic – the leaders, that is, not the people – it includes Denmark (with popular opinion on the war about the same as Germany, therefore 'old Europe'), Portugal (53% opposed to war under any circumstances, 96% opposed to war by the US and its allies unilaterally), Britain (40% opposed to war under any circumstances, 90% opposed to war by the US and its allies unilaterally), and Hungary (no figures available).

In brief, the exciting 'new Europe' consists of some leaders who are willing to defy their populations.

Old Europe reacted with some annoyance to Rumsfeld's declaration that they are 'problem' countries, not modern states. Their reaction was explained by thoughtful United States commentators. Keeping just to the national press, we learn that 'world-weary European allies' do not appreciate the 'moral rectitude' of the President. The evidence for his 'moral rectitude' is that 'his advisors say the evangelical zeal' comes directly from the simple man who is dedicated to driving evil from the world. Since that is surely the most reliable and objective evidence that can be imagined, it would be improper to express slight scepticism, let alone to react as we would to similar performances by others. The cynical Europeans, we are told, misinterpret Bush's purity of soul as 'moral *naïveté*' – without a thought that the administration's public relations specialists might have a hand in creating imagery that will sell. We are informed further that there is a great divide between world-weary Europe and the 'idealistic New World bent on ending inhumanity.' That this is the driving purpose of the idealistic New World we also know for certain, because so our leaders proclaim. What more in the way of proof could one seek?

The rare mention of public opinion in the new Europe treats it as a problem of marketing; the product being sold is necessarily right and honourable, given its source. The willingness of the leaders of the new Europe to prefer Washington to their own populations 'threatens to isolate the Germans and French,' who are exhibiting retrograde democratic tendencies, and shows that Germany and France cannot 'say that they are speaking for Europe.' They are merely speaking for the people of old and new Europe, who – the same commentators acknowledge – express 'strong opposition' to the policies of the new Europe.

The official pronouncements and the reaction to them are illuminating. They demonstrate with some clarity the contempt for democracy that is rather typical, historically, among those who feel that they rule the world by right.

There are many other illustrations. When German Chancellor Gerhard Schroeder dared to take the position of the overwhelming majority of voters in the last election, that was described as a shocking failure of leadership, a serious problem that Germany must overcome if it wants to be accepted in the civilised world. The problem lies with Germany, not élites of the Anglo-American democracies. Germany's problem is that 'the government lives in fear of the voters, and that is causing it to make mistake after mistake' – the spokesperson for the right-wing Christian Social Union party, who understands the real nature of democracy.

The case of Turkey is even more revealing. As throughout the region, Turks are very strongly opposed to the war – about 90% according to the most recent polls. And so far the government has irresponsibly paid some attention to the people who elected it. It has not bowed completely to the intense pressure and threats that Washington is exerting to compel it to heed the master's voice. This reluctance of the elected government to follow orders from on high proves that its leaders are not true democrats. For those who may be too dull to comprehend these subtleties, they are explained by former Ambassador to Turkey Morton Abramowitz, now a distinguished senior statesman and commentator. Ten years ago, he explained, Turkey was governed by a real democrat, Turgut Ozal, who 'overrode his countrymen's pronounced preference to stay out of the Gulf War.' But democracy has declined in Turkey. The current leadership 'is following the people,' revealing its lack of 'democratic credentials.' 'Regrettably,' he says, 'for the United States there is no Ozal around.' So it will be necessary to bring authentic democracy to Turkey by economic strangulation and other coercive means – regrettably, but that is demanded by what the élite press calls our 'yearning for democracy.'

Brazil is witnessing another exercise of the real attitudes towards democracy among the masters of the universe. In the most free election in the hemisphere, a large majority voted for policies that are strongly opposed by international finance and investors, by the International Monetary Fund and the United States Treasury Department. In earlier years, that would have been the signal for a military coup installing a murderous National Security State, as in Brazil 40 years ago. Now that will not work; the populations of South and North have changed, and will not easily tolerate it. Furthermore, there are now simpler ways to undermine the will of the people, thanks to the neo-liberal instruments that have been put in place: economic controls, capital flight, attacks on currency, privatisation, and other devices that are well-designed to reduce the arena of popular choice. These, it is hoped, may compel the government to follow the dictates of what international economists call the 'virtual parliament' of investors and lenders, who make the real decisions, coercing the population, an irrelevant nuisance according to the reigning principles of democracy.

When I was just about to leave for the airport I received another of the many inquiries from the press about why there is so little anti-war protest in the United States. The impressions are instructive. In fact, protest in the United States, as elsewhere, is also at levels that have no historical precedent. Not just demonstrations, teach-ins, and other public events. To take an example of a different kind, last week the Chicago City Council passed an anti-war resolution, 46-1, joining 50 other cities and towns. The same is true in other sectors, including those that are the most highly trusted, as the World Economic Forum learned to its dismay: non-governmental organisations and religious organisations and figures, with few exceptions. Several months ago the biggest university in the country passed a strong anti-war resolution – the University of Texas, right next door to George W's ranch. And it's easy to continue.

So why the widespread judgement among élites that the tradition of dissent and protest has died? Invariably, comparisons are drawn to Vietnam, a very revealing fact. We have just passed the 40th anniversary of the public announcement that the Kennedy administration was sending the United States Air Force to bomb South Vietnam, also initiating plans to drive millions of people into concentration camps and chemical warfare programmes to destroy food crops. There was no pretext of defence, except in the sense of official rhetoric: defence against the 'internal aggression' of South Vietnamese in South Vietnam and their 'assault from the inside' (President Kennedy and his United Nations Ambassador, Adlai Stevenson). Protest was non-existent. It did not reach any meaningful level for several years. By that time hundreds of thousands of United States troops had joined the occupying army, densely-populated areas were being demolished by saturation bombing, and the aggression had spread to the rest of Indochina. Protest among élite intellectuals kept primarily to 'pragmatic grounds': the war was a 'mistake' that was becoming too costly to the United States. In sharp contrast, by the late 1960s the great majority of the public had come to oppose the war as 'fundamentally wrong and immoral,' not 'a mistake,' figures that hold steady until the present.

Today, in dramatic contrast to the 1960s, there is large-scale, committed, and principled popular protest all over the United States before the war has been officially launched. That reflects a steady increase over these years in unwillingness to tolerate aggression and atrocities, one of many such changes, world-wide in fact. That's part of the background for what is taking place in Porto Alegre, and part of the reason for the gloom in Davos.

The political leadership is well aware of these developments. When a new administration comes into office, it receives a review of the world situation compiled by the intelligence agencies. It is secret; we learn about these things many years later. But when Bush no. 1 came into office in 1989, a small part of the review was leaked, a passage concerned with 'cases where the United States confronts much weaker enemies' – the only kind one would think of fighting. Intelligence analysts advised that in conflicts with 'much weaker enemies' the United States must win 'decisively and rapidly,' or popular support will collapse. It's not like the 1960s, when the population would tolerate a murderous and destructive war for years without visible protest. That's no longer true. The activist movements of the past 40 years have had a significant civilizing effect. By now, the only way to attack a much weaker enemy is to construct a huge propaganda offensive depicting it as about to commit genocide, maybe even a threat to our very survival, then to celebrate a miraculous victory over the awesome foe, while chanting praises to the courageous leaders who came to the rescue just in time.

That is the current scenario in Iraq.

Polls reveal more support for the planned war in the United States than elsewhere, but the numbers are misleading. It is important to bear in mind that the United States is the only country outside Iraq where Saddam Hussein is not only reviled but also feared. There is a flood of lurid propaganda warning that if we do not stop him today he will destroy us tomorrow. The next evidence of his weapons of mass destruction may be a 'mushroom cloud,' so National Security Adviser Condoleeza Rice announced in September – presumably over New York. No one in Iraq's neighbourhood seems overly concerned, much as they may hate the murderous tyrant. Perhaps that is because they know that as a result of the sanctions 'the vast majority of the country's population has been on a semi-starvation diet for years,' as the World Health Organisation reported, and that Iraq is one of the weakest states in the region: its economy and military expenditures are a fraction of Kuwait's, which has 10% of Iraq's population, and much farther below others nearby.

But the United States is different. When Congress granted the President authority to go to war last October, it was 'to defend the national security of the United States against the continuing threat posed by Iraq.' We must tremble in fear before this awesome threat, while countries nearby seek to reintegrate Iraq into the region, including those who were attacked by Saddam when he was a friend and ally of those who now run the show in Washington – and who were happily providing him with aid, including the means to develop weapons of mass destruction, at a time when he was far more dangerous than today and had already committed by far his worst crimes.

A serious measure of support for war in the United States would have to extricate this 'fear factor,' which is genuine, and unique to the United States. The residue would give a more realistic measure of support for the resort to violence, and would show, I think, that it is about the same as elsewhere.

It is also rather striking that strong opposition to the coming war extends right through the establishment. The current issues of the two major foreign policy journals feature articles opposing the war by leading figures of foreign policy élites. The very respectable American Academy of Arts and Sciences released a long monograph on the war, trying to give the most sympathetic possible account of the Bush administration position, then dismantling it point by point. One respected analyst they quote is a Senior Associate of the Carnegie Endowment for International Peace, who warns that the United States is becoming 'a menace to itself and to mankind' under its current leadership. There are no precedents for anything like this.

We should recognize that these criticisms tend to be narrow. They are concerned with threats to the United States and its allies. They do not take into account the likely effects on Iraqis: the warnings of the United Nations and aid agencies that millions may be at very serious risk in a country that is at the edge of survival after a terrible war that targeted its basic infrastructure – which amounts to biological warfare – and a decade of devastating sanctions that have killed hundreds of thousands of people and blocked any reconstruction, while strengthening the brutal tyrant who rules Iraq. It is also interesting that the criticisms do not even take the trouble to mention the lofty rhetoric about democratisation and liberation. Presumably, the critics take for granted that the rhetoric is intended for intellectuals and editorial writers – who are not supposed to notice that the drive to war is accompanied by a dramatic demonstration of hatred of democracy, just as they are supposed to forget the record of those who are leading the campaign. That is also why none of this is ever brought up at the United Nations.

Nevertheless, the threats that do concern establishment critics are very real. They were surely not surprised when the CIA informed Congress last October that they know of no link between Iraq and Al Qaeda-style terrorism, but that an attack on Iraq would probably increase the terrorist threat to the West, in many ways. It is likely to inspire a new generation of terrorists bent on revenge, and it might induce Iraq to carry out terrorist actions that are already in place, a possibility taken very seriously by United States analysts. A high-level task force of the Council on Foreign Relations just released a report warning of likely terrorist attacks that could be far worse than 9/11, including possible use of weapons of mass destruction right within the United States, dangers that become 'more urgent by the prospect of the United States going to war with Iraq.' They provide many illustrations, virtually a cook-book for terrorists. It is not the first; similar ones were published by prominent strategic analysts long before 9/11.

It is also understood that an attack on Iraq may lead not just to more terror, but also to proliferation of weapons of mass destruction, for a simple reason: potential targets of the United States recognise that there is no other way to deter the most powerful state in history, which is pursuing 'America's Imperial Ambition,' posing serious dangers to the United States and the world, the author warns in the main establishment journal, *Foreign Affairs*. Prominent hawks warn that a war in Iraq might lead to the 'greatest proliferation disaster in history.' They know that if Iraq has chemical and biological weapons, the dictatorship keeps them under tight control. They understand further that except as a last resort if attacked, Iraq is highly unlikely to use any weapon of mass destruction it has, thus inviting instant incineration. And it is also highly unlikely to leak them to the Osama bin Ladens of the world, which would be a terrible threat to Saddam Hussein himself, quite apart from the reaction if there is even a hint that this might take place. But under attack, the society would collapse, including the controls over weapons of mass destruction. These would be 'privatised,' terrorism experts point out, and offered to the huge 'market for unconventional weapons, where they will have no trouble finding buyers.' That really is a 'nightmare scenario,' just as the hawks warn.

Even before the Bush administration began beating the war drums about Iraq, there were plenty of warnings that its adventurism was going to lead to proliferation of weapons of mass destruction, as well as terror, simply as a deterrent. Right now, Washington is teaching the world a very ugly and dangerous lesson: if you want to defend yourself from us, you had better mimic North Korea and pose a credible military threat, including weapons of mass destruction. Otherwise we will demolish you in pursuit of the new 'grand strategy' that has caused shudders not only among the usual victims, and in 'old Europe,' but right at the heart of the United States foreign policy élite, who recognise that 'commitment of the United States to active military confrontation for decisive national advantage will leave the world more dangerous and the United States less secure' – again, quoting respected figures in élite journals.

Evidently, the likely increase of terror and proliferation of weapons of mass destruction is of limited concern to planners in Washington, in the context of their real priorities. Without too much difficulty, one can think of reasons why this might be the case, not very attractive ones.

The nature of the threats was dramatically underscored last October, at the summit meeting in Havana on the 40th anniversary of the Cuban missile crisis, attended by key participants from Russia, the United States, and Cuba. Planners knew at the time that they had the fate of the world in their hands, but new information released at the Havana summit was truly startling. We learned that the world was saved from nuclear devastation by one Russian submarine captain,

Vasily Arkhipov, who blocked an order to fire nuclear missiles when Russian submarines were attacked by United States destroyers near Kennedy's 'quarantine' line. Had Arkhipov agreed, the nuclear launch would have almost certainly set off an interchange that could have 'destroyed the Northern hemisphere,' as Eisenhower had warned.

The dreadful revelation is particularly timely because of the circumstances: the roots of the missile crisis lay in international terrorism aimed at 'regime change,' two concepts very much in the news today. US terrorist attacks against Cuba began shortly after Castro took power, and were sharply escalated by Kennedy, leading to a very plausible fear of invasion, as Robert McNamara has acknowledged. Kennedy resumed the terrorist war immediately after the crisis was over; terrorist actions against Cuba, based in the United States, peaked in the late 1970s and continued 20 years later. Putting aside any judgement about the behaviour of the participants in the missile crisis, the new discoveries demonstrate with brilliant clarity the terrible and unanticipated risks of attacks on a 'much weaker enemy' aimed at 'regime change' – risks to survival, it is no exaggeration to say.

As for the fate of the people of Iraq, no one can predict with any confidence: not the Central Intelligence Agency, not Donald Rumsfeld, not those who claim to be experts on Iraq, no one. Possibilities range from the frightening prospects for which the aid agencies are preparing, to the delightful tales spun by administration public relations specialists and their chorus. One never knows. These are among the many reasons why decent human beings do not contemplate the threat or use of violence, whether in personal life or international affairs, unless reasons have been offered that have overwhelming force. And surely nothing remotely like that has been offered in the present case, which is why opposition to the plans of Washington and London has reached such scale and intensity.

The timing of the Washington-London propaganda campaign was so transparent that it too has been a topic of discussion, and sometimes ridicule, right in the mainstream. The campaign began in September of last year. Before that, Saddam was a terrible guy, but not an imminent threat to the survival of the US. The 'mushroom cloud' was announced in early September. Since then, fear that Saddam will attack the United States has been running at about 60-70% of the population. 'The desperate urgency about moving rapidly against Iraq that Bush expressed in October was not evident from anything he said two months before,' the chief political analyst of United Press International observed, drawing the obvious conclusion: September marked the opening of the political campaign for the mid-term congressional elections. The administration, he continued, was 'campaigning to sustain and increase its power on a policy of international adventurism, new radical pre-emptive military strategies, and a hunger for a politically convenient and perfectly timed confrontation with Iraq.' As long as domestic issues were in the forefront, Bush and his cohorts were losing ground – naturally enough, because they are conducting a serious assault against the general population. 'But lo and behold! Though there have been no new terrorist attacks or credible indications of imminent threat, since the beginning of September, national security issues have been in the driver's seat,' not just Al Qaeda but an awesome and threatening military power, Iraq.

The same observations have been made by many others. That's convenient for people like us: we can just quote the mainstream instead of giving controversial analyses. The Carnegie Endowment Senior Associate I quoted before writes that Bush and Co. are following 'the classic modern strategy of an endangered right-wing oligarchy, which is to divert mass discontent into nationalism,' inspired by fear of enemies about to destroy us. That strategy is of critical importance if the 'radical nationalists' setting policy in Washington hope to advance their announced plan for 'unilateral world domination through absolute military superiority,' while conducting a major assault against the interests of the large majority of the domestic population.

For the elections, the strategy worked, barely. The Fall 2002 election was won by a small number of votes, but enough to hand Congress to the executive. Analyses of the election found that voters maintained their opposition to the administration on social and economic issues, but suppressed these issues in favour of security concerns, which typically lead to support for the figure in authority – the brave cowboy who must ride to our rescue, just in time.

As history shows, it is all too easy for unscrupulous leaders to terrify the public, with consequences that have not been attractive. That is the natural method to divert attention from the fact that tax cuts for the rich and other devices are undermining prospects for a decent life for the large majority of the population, and for future generations. When the presidential campaign begins, Republican strategists surely do not want people to be asking questions about their pensions, jobs, health care, and other such matters. Rather, they should be praising their heroic leader for rescuing them from imminent destruction by a foe of colossal power, and marching on to confront the next powerful force bent on our destruction. It could be Iran, or conflicts in the Andean countries: there are lots of good choices, as long as the targets are defenceless.

These ideas are second nature to the current political leaders, most of them recycled from the Reagan administration. They are replaying a familiar script: drive the country into deficit so as to be able to undermine social programmes, declare a 'war on terror' (as they did in 1981) and conjure up one devil after another to frighten the population into obedience. In the 1980s it was Libyan hit-men prowling the streets of Washington to assassinate our leader, then the Nicaraguan army only two-days march from Texas, a threat to survival so severe that Reagan had to declare a national emergency. Or an airfield in Grenada that the Russians were going to use to bomb us (if they could find it on a map); Arab terrorists seeking to kill Americans everywhere while Qaddafi plans to 'expel America from the world,' so Reagan wailed. Or Hispanic narco-traffickers seeking to destroy the youth; and on, and on.

Meanwhile the political leadership were able to carry out domestic policies that had generally poor economic outcomes but did create wealth for narrow sectors while harming a considerable majority of the population – the script that is being followed once again. And since the public knows it, they have to resort to 'the classic modern strategy of an endangered right wing oligarchy' if they hope to carry out the domestic and international programmes to which they are committed, perhaps even to institutionalise them so they will be hard to dismantle when they lose control.

Of course, there is much more to it than domestic considerations – which are of no slight importance in themselves. The September 11 terrorist atrocities provided an opportunity and pretext to implement long-standing plans to take control of Iraq's immense oil wealth, a central component of the Persian Gulf resources that the State Department, in 1945, described as 'a stupendous source of strategic power, and one of the greatest material prizes in world history.' US intelligence predicts that these will be of even greater significance in the years ahead. The issue has never been access. The same intelligence analyses anticipate that the United States will rely on more secure supplies in the Western hemisphere and West Africa. The same was true after World War Two. What matters is control over the 'material prize,' which funnels enormous wealth to the United States in many ways, Britain as well, and the 'stupendous source of strategic power,' which translates into a lever of 'unilateral world domination' – the goal that is now openly proclaimed, and is frightening much of the world, including 'old Europe' and the conservative establishment in the United States.

I think a realistic look at the world gives a mixed picture. There are many reasons to be encouraged, but there will be a long hard road ahead.

Confronting Empire

Arundhati Roy

Arundhati Roy, the Booker Prize-winning author of The God of Small Things, *is a foremost campaigner against war, particularly in India. Her speech to the World Social Forum was heard by an estimated audience of eighteen thousand people.*

I've been asked to speak about 'How to confront Empire?' It's a huge question, and I have no easy answers.

When we speak of confronting 'Empire,' we need to identify what 'Empire' means. Does it mean the United States government (and its European satellites), the World Bank, the International Monetary Fund, the World Trade Organisation, and multinational corporations? Or is it something more than that?

In many countries, Empire has sprouted other subsidiary heads, some dangerous by-products – nationalism, religious bigotry, fascism and, of course, terrorism. All these march arm in arm with the project of corporate globalisation.

Let me illustrate what I mean. India – the world's biggest democracy – is currently at the forefront of the corporate globalisation project. Its 'market' of one billion people is being prized open by the World Trade Organisation. Corporatisation and privatisation are being welcomed by the government and the Indian elite. It is not a coincidence that the Prime Minister, the Home Minister, the Disinvestment Minister – the men who signed the deal with Enron in India, the men who are selling the country's infrastructure to corporate multinationals, the men who want to privatise water, electricity, oil, coal, steel, health, education and telecommunication – are all members or admirers of the RSS. The RSS is a right wing, ultra-nationalist Hindu guild which has openly admired Hitler and his methods.

The dismantling of democracy is proceeding with the speed and efficiency of a Structural Adjustment Programme. While the project of corporate globalisation rips through people's lives in India, massive privatisation, and labour 'reforms' are pushing people off their land and out of their jobs. Hundreds of impoverished farmers are committing suicide by consuming pesticide. Reports of starvation deaths are coming in from all over the country. While the élite journeys to its imaginary destination somewhere near the top of the world, the dispossessed are spiralling downwards into crime and chaos. This climate of frustration and national disillusionment is the perfect breeding ground, history tells us, for fascism.

The two arms of the Indian Government have evolved the perfect pincer action. While one arm is busy selling India off in chunks, the other, to divert attention, is orchestrating a howling, baying chorus of Hindu nationalism and religious fascism. It is conducting nuclear tests, rewriting history books, burning churches, and demolishing mosques. Censorship, surveillance, the suspension of civil liberties and human rights, the definition of who is an Indian citizen and who is not, particularly with regard to religious minorities, is becoming common practice now.

Last March, in the state of Gujarat, two thousand Muslims were butchered in a state-sponsored pogrom. Muslim women were specially targeted. They were stripped, and gang-raped, before being burned alive. Arsonists burned and looted shops, homes, textiles mills, and mosques. More than a hundred and fifty thousand Muslims have been driven from their homes. The economic base of the Muslim community has been devastated.

While Gujarat burned, the Indian Prime Minister was on MTV promoting his new poems. In January this year, the Government that orchestrated the killing was voted back into office with a comfortable majority. Nobody has been punished for the genocide. Narendra Modi, architect of the pogrom, proud member of the RSS, has embarked on his second term as the Chief Minister of Gujarat. If he were Saddam Hussein, of course, each atrocity would have been on CNN. But since he's not – and since the Indian 'market' is open to global investors – the massacre is not even an embarrassing inconvenience.

There are more than one hundred million Muslims in India. A time bomb is ticking in our ancient land.

All this to say that it is a myth that the free market breaks down national barriers. The free market does not threaten national sovereignty, it undermines democracy. As the disparity between the rich and the poor grows, the fight to corner resources is intensifying. To push through their 'sweetheart deals,' to corporatise the crops we grow, the water we drink, the air we breathe, and the dreams we dream, corporate globalisation needs an international confederation of loyal, corrupt, authoritarian governments in poorer countries to push through unpopular reforms and quell the mutinies.

Corporate globalisation – or shall we call it by its name? – imperialism – needs a press that pretends to be free. It needs courts that pretend to dispense justice. Meanwhile, the countries of the North harden their borders and stockpile weapons of mass destruction. After all they have to make sure that it's only money, goods, patents and services that are globalised. Not the free movement of people. Not a respect for human rights. Not international treaties on racial discrimination or chemical and nuclear weapons or greenhouse gas emissions or climate change, or – god forbid – justice.

So this – all this – is 'empire.' This loyal confederation, this obscene accumulation of power, this greatly increased distance between those who make the decisions and those who have to suffer them. Our fight, our goal, our vision of Another World must be to eliminate that distance. So how do we resist 'Empire'?

The good news is that we're not doing too badly. There have been major victories. Here in Latin America you have had so many – in Bolivia, you have Cochabamba. In Peru, there was the uprising in Arequipa. In Venezuela, President Hugo Chavez is holding on, despite the United States government's best efforts. And the world's gaze is on the people of Argentina, who are trying to refashion a country from the ashes of the havoc wrought by the International Monetary Fund.

In India the movement against corporate globalisation is gathering momentum and is poised to become the only real political force to counter religious fascism. As for corporate globalisation's glittering ambassadors – Enron, Bechtel, WorldCom, Arthur Anderson – where were they last year, and where are they now? And of course here in Brazil we must ask …who was the president last year, and who is it now?

Still … many of us have dark moments of hopelessness and despair. We know that under the spreading canopy of the War Against Terrorism, the men in suits are hard at work. While bombs rain down on us, and cruise missiles skid across the skies, we know that contracts are being signed, patents are being registered, oil pipelines are being laid, natural resources are being plundered, water is being privatised, and George Bush is planning to go to war against Iraq.

If we look at this conflict as a straightforward eye-ball to eye-ball confrontation between 'Empire' and those of us who are resisting it, it might seem that we are losing. But there is another way of looking at it. We, all of us gathered here, have, each in our own way, laid siege to 'Empire.' We may not have stopped it in its tracks – yet – but we have stripped it down. We have made it drop its mask. We have forced it into the open. It now stands before us on the world's stage in all it's brutish, iniquitous nakedness.

Empire may well go to war, but it's out in the open now – too ugly to behold its own reflection. Too ugly even to rally its own people. It won't be long before the majority of American people become our allies. Only a few days ago in Washington, a quarter of a million people marched against the war on Iraq. Each month, the protest is gathering momentum.

Before September 11th 2001 America had a secret history. Secret especially from its own people. But now America's secrets are history, and its history is public knowledge. It's street talk. Today, we know that every argument that is being used to escalate the war against Iraq is a lie. The most ludicrous of them being the United States government's deep commitment to bring democracy to Iraq.

Killing people to save them from dictatorship or ideological corruption is, of course, an old United States government sport. Here in Latin America, you know that better than most. Nobody doubts that Saddam Hussein is a ruthless dictator, a murderer (whose worst excesses were supported by the governments of the United States and Great Britain). There's no doubt that Iraqis would be better off without him. But, then, the whole world would be better off without a certain Mr. Bush. In fact, he is far more dangerous than Saddam Hussein.

So, should we bomb Bush out of the White House? It's more than clear that Bush is determined to go to war against Iraq, regardless of the facts – and regardless of international public opinion. In its recruitment drive for allies, the United States is prepared to invent facts. The charade with weapons inspectors is the United States government's offensive, insulting concession to some twisted form of international etiquette. It's like leaving the 'doggie door' open for last minute 'allies' or maybe the United Nations to crawl through.

But for all intents and purposes, the New War against Iraq has begun. What can we do? We can hone our memory, we can learn from our history. We can continue to build public opinion until it becomes a deafening roar. We can turn the war on Iraq into a fishbowl of the United States government's excesses. We can expose George Bush and Tony Blair – and their allies – for the cowardly baby killers, water poisoners, and pusillanimous long-distance bombers that they are. We can re-invent civil disobedience in a million different ways. In other words, we can come up with a million ways of becoming a collective pain in the ass.

When George Bush says 'you're either with us, or you are with the terrorists' we can say 'No thank you.' We can let him know that the people of the world do not need to choose between a Malevolent Mickey Mouse and the Mad Mullahs. Our strategy should be not only to confront empire, but to lay siege to it. To deprive it of oxygen. To shame it. To mock it. With our art, our music, our literature, our stubbornness, our joy, our brilliance, our sheer relentlessness – and our ability to tell our own stories. Stories that are different from the ones we're being brainwashed to believe.

The corporate revolution will collapse if we refuse to buy what they are selling – their ideas, their version of history, their wars, their weapons, their notion of inevitability. Remember this: We be many and they be few. They need us more than we need them. Another world is not only possible, she is on her way. On a quiet day, I can hear her breathing.

This is an article by Arundhati Roy ©Arundhati Roy 2003.

Full Spectrum Democracy

Ken Coates

The imminent war on Iraq will probably destroy that country, although the process could possibly take longer than the Americans and British appear to think. However that may be, it is also likely to undermine the credibility of the United Nations as a system of international law and world governance.

American diplomats have certainly accomplished short-term miracles of persuasion in securing the agreement of the Security Council to resolution 1441. But all the backstairs intrigue will become a negative quantity as it is subjected to the glare of daylight publicity, during the attempts to provide a pretext for war. If the Security Council loses what moral authority it used to have, other institutions are also jeopardised. Already the predatory doctrine of counter-proliferation is supplanting the careful agreements that were involved in nuclear non-proliferation, substituting brute force for conviction, even though such force has never been sanctioned by any duly constituted authority. The Non-proliferation Treaty has functioned imperfectly, but where it has worked it has represented a victory for persuasion and understanding. Counter-proliferation has opposed those processes, substituting the brute compulsion of the stronger. The rule of the strong encourages cunning and sycophancy, not peace.

We have already drawn attention to the fact that resolution 1441 imposed upon the Iraqis the duty of presenting a comprehensive report on their preparations for the manufacture of weapons of mass destruction, as well as on any present stocks which they may have. It rapidly became known that the Americans intercepted the resultant Iraqi dossier when it was handed over to the United Nations. What has not been widely reported is that more than 8,000 pages of this dossier (out of 11,800 pages) were suppressed when the meagre residuum was made available to non-permanent members of the Security Council. Thus such members will never see the vast majority of the evidence which

Ken Coates is Editor of The Spokesman and Chairman of the Bertrand Russell Peace Foundation.

the Iraqis have submitted for their consideration (see Peace Dossier page 71).

Meantime, the weapons inspectorate report two 'finds' on the ground in Iraq. The first consists of eleven empty shell cases, and could only be taken seriously by people who were deranged. The second consists of voluminous notes belonging to an Iraqi professor. Had these already been declared? In the light of the suppression of more than 8,000 pages of an 11,800 page dossier, it will be hard to know. But in this case non-compliance is an action of the US administration, not the Iraqis.

The United States is militarily the preponderant world power. Economically, it also has considerable clout, although this is less far-reaching than is sometimes assumed. But the arbitrary usurpation of decisions which properly belong to others is detonating an overwhelming movement of worldwide resistance, which represents a potentially far greater power than all that awesome military force.

American primacy had been emerging before the end of the Cold war, and was theorised by Zbigniew Brzezinski in his influential tract: *The Grand Chessboard*. Brzezinski had been President Carter's National Security Advisor in Afghanistan, through the confrontation with the Russians in which the United States played a major role. Here it was that the first volunteer Arabs raised the flag of Islam against the Russian invaders. Brzezinski wrote to Carter to insist that the Russians could be defeated in Afghanistan, thus, he thought, redressing the American defeat in Vietnam which weighed so heavily on the self-image of American leaders. More: Brzezinski began to draw wider lessons:

> '... how America 'manages' Eurasia is critical. Eurasia is the globe's largest continent and is geopolitically axial. A power that dominates Eurasia would control two of the world's three most advanced and economically productive regions ... About 75 per cent of the world's people live in Eurasia, and most of the world's physical wealth is there as well ... Eurasia accounts for about 60 per cent of the world's GNP and about three-fourths of the world's known energy resources... Eurasia is thus the chessboard on which the struggle for global primacy continues to be played.'[1]

The rules of the new chess game are altogether very different from the old rules, however. For Brzezinski,

> 'Eurasian geostrategy involves the purposeful management of geostrategically dynamic states and the careful handling of geopolitically catalytic states, in keeping with the twin interests of America in the short-term preservation of its unique global power and in the long-run transformation of it into increasingly institutionalized global cooperation. To put it in a terminology that hearkens back to the more brutal age of ancient empires, the three grand imperatives of imperial geostrategy are to prevent collusion and maintain security dependence among the vassals, to keep tributaries pliant and protected, and to keep the barbarians from coming together.'[2]

Extrapolating from this theme, Brzezinski told us that for the Americans,

> 'The most dangerous scenario would be a grand coalition of China, Russia, and perhaps Iran, an 'antihegemonic coalition united not by ideology but by complementary grievances'.'[3]

Alongside this bold political project, the American military devised the brutally clear doctrine of 'Full Spectrum Dominance'.

> 'The ultimate goal of our military force is to accomplish the objectives directed by the National Command Authorities. For the joint force of the future, this goal will be achieved through full spectrum dominance – the ability of US forces operating unilaterally or in combination with multinational and interagency partners, to defeat any adversary and control any situation across the full range of military operations.
>
> The full range of operations includes maintaining a posture of strategic deterrence. It includes theatre engagement and presence activities. It includes conflict involving employment of strategic forces and weapons of mass destruction, major theatre wars, regional conflicts, and smaller-scale contingencies. It also includes those ambiguous situations residing between peace and war, such as peacekeeping and peace enforcement operations, as well as non-combat humanitarian relief operations and support to domestic authorities.
>
> The label full spectrum dominance implies that US forces are able to conduct prompt, sustained, and synchronised operations with combinations of forces tailored to specific situations and with access to and freedom to operate in all domains – space, sea, land, air, and information. Additionally, given the global nature of our interests and obligations, the United States must maintain its overseas presence forces and the ability to rapidly project power world-wide in order to achieve full spectrum dominance.'[4]

The use of such power can be fine-tuned, as Colonel John A. Warden II of the US Air Force, explains in his paper 'The Enemy as a System'[5]. This represents a thorough-going revision of the thinking of Clausewitz and Napoleon, and begins with a severely rational examination of how to achieve the objectives of the United States.

> 'At the strategic level', says Colonel Warden, 'we attain our objectives by causing such changes to one or more parts of the enemy's physical system that the enemy decides to adopt our objectives, or we make it physically impossible for him to oppose us. The latter we call strategic paralysis. Which parts of the enemy system we attack ... will depend on what our objectives are, how much the enemy wants to resist us, how capable he is, and how much effort we are physically, morally, and politically capable of exercising.'

But what is the enemy 'system'? Warden offers a simplified model of five rings. At the centre is the leadership or brain. In the next circle are the organic essentials, food, energy, and so on. Thirdly, there is the infrastructure, of vital connections and skeletal essentials: roads, air fields, factories, transmission lines. The fourth ring is the population which is sustained by these essentials, and is necessary to sustain them. Lastly, and in fact least important for many purposes, is the circle of the fighting mechanism.

The purpose of modern war is not to confront arms, or kill soldiers. If this process could be avoided altogether, that would be fine by the controllers of modern war, provided only that they could exercise their will over enough of the other rings to bend the enemy leadership to their own purposes.

Colonel Warden explains these categories with a series of intricate diagrams. But such diagrams are not necessary for us to realise that within this model, American Generals do not think about conventional battlefield conquest. What they care about is the destruction of the enemy system, if not by the liquidation of its leadership, then by cumulative damage to the essentials which sustain it.

> 'We must not start our thinking on war with the tools of war – with the air planes, tanks, ships and those who crew them. These tools are important and have their place, but they cannot be our starting point, nor can we allow ourselves to see them as the essentials of war. Fighting is not the essence of war, nor even a desirable part of it. The real essence is doing what is necessary to make the enemy accept our objectives as his objectives.'

All this adds up to a fairly clear imperial charter. If it took time to arrive in the understanding of European political leaders, this was partly because it was accompanied by attempts to revise the constitution of Nato, and by the hope that Brzezinski's goal of 'long-run transformation ... into increasingly institutionalized global cooperation' might be part of a mutually acceptable world order, if only for the rich countries, the old imperial powers.

The advent of George Bush put paid to this hope, which was always somewhat platonic. Firstly, the new President made short work of declaring his right to pre-emptive action. His Nuclear Posture Review made chilling assumptions of the need for first strike nuclear strategies. He wasted no time in indulging the consensus of lesser States about the need for global co-operation to prevent damage to the environment, and at once repudiated the Kyoto protocols outright. Not only did he greet the proposals for an International Criminal Court as unacceptable, but he immediately embarked upon a series of measures aimed at sabotaging any powers which the Court might claim in order to judge American citizens. These and a series of other actions, including the unilateral repudiation of Treaties, made it impossible to believe that the President shared Brzezinski's desire for internationally institutionalised global co-operation, on any other basis than that of naked imperial power. All this comes to a head in the American decision to attack Iraq, with the blessing of a cowed and fearful United Nations if it is available, but on its unilateral initiative if not. Detailed plans were announced to install General Tommy Franks as the controller of occupied Iraq, explicitly modelling his anticipated regime on that of General MacArthur in occupied Japan after 1945. Various other proposals have been canvassed involving a number of other nominees.

Evidently, the factional differences within the American political and military establishments have not resolved themselves. But the destruction of the Iraqi Government will not be likely to moderate belligerence, either in the Bush administration, or even in any foreseeable replacement, until the peace movement in the United States can assert itself.

After Iraq, there is the unresolved problem of Korea, which may not be brought to a head quickly, because it seems that the United States is not yet ready to take on the task of destroying China. But once it is installed in Baghdad, the likelihood of further military adventures in the Middle East becomes greater, not smaller. Iran is an old adversary to the American establishment. The likely turbulence which will break out in the Arabian peninsula may well invite military responses from the Americans, though this will terrify some of their British allies.

Meantime concern all around the world extends far beyond the numbers of convinced pacifists or even the critics of the misdeeds done in the name of globalism.

Full Spectrum Dominance commends itself to builders of empires because it seems to be as permanent as they think their ugly monuments to be. But nothing is less permanent than domination. It is more evanescent than the fear and misery it generates. We should remember Shelley's Ozymandias, or Ramses III. The poet came across the ruins of a great monument in the desert: he found 'two vast and trunkless legs of stone' and 'a half-sunk shattered visage'. Nearby, there stood a pedestal which said:

'My name is Ozymandias, king of kings;
Look on my works, ye Mighty, and despair!'

But that was all...

'Nothing beside remains. Round the decay
Of that colossal wreck, boundless and bare
The lone and level sands stretch far away.'

What may be hoped to be more permanent than domination is the antidote it will generate: human sympathy, creativity, solidarity. That is why, if the Porto Alegre process did not exist, we should have to invent it.

Footnotes

1 *The Grand Chessboard*, Basic Books, New York, 1997.
2 Ibid, p.40.
3 Ibid, p.55
4 United States Department of Defence: *Joint Vision 2020*, 30th May 2000.
5 'The Enemy as a System' can be located on the internet at
  http://www.airpower.au.af.mil/airchronicles/apj/warden.html

Kurt Vonnegut *versus* the !&#*!@

Kurt Vonnegut gave us a pamphlet in 1982 which is still much sought after in the peace movement. It is called Fates Worse Than Death *(available from Spokesman Books). Here, he answers Joel Bleifuss's questions about the war on Iraq. With grateful acknowledgements to* In These Times *magazine.*

In November 2002, Kurt Vonnegut turned 80. He published his first novel, *Player Piano*, in 1952 at the age of 29. Since then he has written 13 others, including *Slaughterhouse Five*, pre-eminent among anti-war novels of the 20th century.

Vonnegut is an American socialist in the tradition of Eugene Victor Debs, a fellow Hoosier whom he likes to quote: 'As long as there is a lower class, I am in it. As long as there is a criminal element, I am of it. As long as there is a soul in prison, I am not free.'

* * *

You have lived through World War Two, Korea, Vietnam, the Reagan wars, Desert Storm, the Balkan wars and now this coming war in Iraq. What has changed, and what has remained the same?

One thing which has not changed is that none of us, no matter what continent or island or ice cap, asked to be born in the first place, and that even somebody as old as I am, which is 80, only just got here. There were already all these games going on when I got here. ... An apt motto for any polity anywhere, to put on its state seal or currency or whatever, might be this quotation from the late baseball manager Casey Stengel, who was addressing a team of losing professional athletes: 'Can't anybody here play this game?'

My daughter Lily, for an example close to home, who has just turned 20, finds herself—as does George W. Bush, himself a kid—an heir to a shockingly recent history of human slavery, to an Aids epidemic and to nuclear submarines slumbering on the floors of fjords in Iceland and elsewhere, crews prepared at a moment's notice to turn industrial quantities of men, women and children into radioactive soot and bonemeal by means of rockets and H-bomb warheads. And to the choice between liberalism or conservatism and on and on.

What is radically new in 2003 is that my daughter, along with our president and Saddam Hussein and on and on, has inherited technologies whose by-products, whether in war or peace, are rapidly destroying the whole planet as a breathable, drinkable system for supporting life of any kind. Human beings, past and present, have trashed the joint.

> *Based on what you've read and seen in the media, what is not being said in the mainstream press about President Bush's policies and the impending war in Iraq?*

That they are nonsense.

> *My feeling from talking to readers and friends is that many people are beginning to despair. Do you think that we've lost reason to hope?*

I myself feel that our country, for whose Constitution I fought in a just war, might as well have been invaded by Martians and body snatchers. Sometimes I wish it had been. What has happened, though, is that it has been taken over by means of the sleaziest, low-comedy, Keystone Cops-style *coup d'état* imaginable. And those now in charge of the federal government are upper-crust C-students who know no history or geography, plus not-so-closeted white supremacists, aka 'Christians,' and plus, most frighteningly, psychopathic personalities, or 'PPs.'

To say somebody is a PP is to make a perfectly respectable medical diagnosis, like saying he or she has appendicitis or athlete's foot. The classic medical text on PPs is *The Mask of Sanity* by Dr. Hervey Cleckley. Read it! PPs are presentable, they know full well the suffering their actions may cause others, but they do not care. They cannot care because they are nuts. They have a screw loose!

And what syndrome better describes so many executives at Enron and WorldCom and on and on, who have enriched themselves while ruining their employees and investors and country, and who still feel as pure as the driven snow, no matter what anybody may say to or about them? And so many of these heartless PPs now hold big jobs in our federal government, as though they were leaders instead of sick.

What has allowed so many PPs to rise so high in corporations, and now in government, is that they are so decisive. Unlike normal people, they are never filled with doubts, for the simple reason that they cannot care what happens next. Simply can't. Do this! Do that! Mobilise the reserves! Privatise the public schools! Attack Iraq! Cut health care! Tap everybody's telephone! Cut taxes on the rich! Build a trillion-dollar missile shield! Fuck *habeas corpus* and the Sierra Club and *In These Times,* and kiss my ass!

> *How have you gotten involved in the anti-war movement? And how would you compare the movement against a war in Iraq with the anti-war movement of the Vietnam era?*

When it became obvious what a dumb and cruel and spiritually and financially and militarily ruinous mistake our war in Vietnam was, every artist worth a damn in this country, every serious writer, painter, stand-up comedian, musician, actor and actress, you name it, came out against the thing. We formed what might be described as a laser beam of protest, with everybody aimed in the same direction, focused and intense. This weapon proved to have the power of a banana-cream pie three feet in diameter when dropped from a stepladder five-feet high.

And so it is with anti-war protests in the present day. Then as now, TV did not like anti-war protesters, nor any other sort of protesters, unless they rioted. Now, as then, on account of TV, the right of citizens to peaceably assemble, and petition their government for a redress of grievances, 'ain't worth a pitcher of warm spit,' as the saying goes.

As a writer and artist, have you noticed any difference between how the cultural leaders of the past and the cultural leaders of today view their responsibility to society?

Responsibility to which society? To Nazi Germany? To the Stalinist Soviet Union? What about responsibility to humanity in general? And leaders in what particular cultural activity? I guess you mean the fine arts. I hope you mean the fine arts. ... Anybody practising the fine art of composing music, no matter how cynical or greedy or scared, still can't help serving all humanity. Music makes practically everybody fonder of life than he or she would be without it. Even military bands, although I am a pacifist, always cheer me up.

But that is the power of ear candy. The creation of such a universal confection for the eye, by means of printed poetry or fiction or history or essays or memoirs and so on, isn't possible. Literature is by definition opinionated. It is bound to provoke the arguments in many quarters, not excluding the hometown or even the family of the author. Any ink-on-paper author can only hope at best to seem responsible to small groups or like-minded people somewhere. He or she might as well have given an interview to the editor of a small-circulation publication.

Maybe we can talk about the responsibilities to their societies of architects and sculptors and painters another time. And I will say this: TV drama, although not yet classified as fine art, has on occasion performed marvellous services for Americans who want us to be less paranoid, to be fairer and more merciful. *M.A.S.H.* and *Law and Order,* to name only two shows, have been stunning masterpieces in that regard.

That said, do you have any ideas for a really scary reality TV show?

'C students from Yale.' It would stand your hair on end.

What targets would you consider fair game for a satirist today?

Assholes.

* * *

The interview led to this exchange of letters.

Dear Mr. Vonnegut,
What genuinely motivates Al Qaeda to kill and self-destruct? The president says, 'They hate our freedoms – our freedom of religion, our freedom of speech, our freedom to vote and assemble and disagree with each other,' which surely is not

what has been learned from the captives being held in Guantanamo, or what he is told in his briefings. Why do the communications industry and our elected politicians allow Bush to get away with such nonsense? And how can there ever be peace, and even trust in our leaders, if the American people aren't told the truth?

Peter Hoyt, Little Deer Island, Maine

Dear Mr. Hoyt,
One wishes that those who have taken over our federal government, and hence the world, by means of a Mickey Mouse *coup d'état*, and who have disconnected all the burglar alarms prescribed by the Constitution, which is to say the House and Senate and the Supreme Court and We the People, were truly Christian. But as William Shakespeare told us long ago, 'The devil can cite Scripture for his purpose.'

And what remains the best-kept secret from the Second World War, because it is so embarrassing, is that Hitler was a Christian, and that his swastika was a Christian cross made of axes, an apt symbol of a political party for Christians of the working class. And there were simpler, unambiguous crosses on all Hitler's tanks and planes.

Again: one wishes, for the sake of the whole planet, that the people in and around the White House nowadays truly mean it when they say, 'Forgive us our trespasses as we forgive those who trespass against us,' and that they respect as children of God the losers, the nobodies so loved by Jesus in the Beatitudes, in His Sermon on the Mount: the poor in spirit, they that mourn, the meek, the merciful, the peace makers and so on.

But such is obviously not the case. George W. Bush smirks and gloats unmercifully as he boasts of his readiness to loose more than a hundred cruise missiles, what I call 'Timothy McVeighs,' into the midst of the general population of Iraq, nearly half of whom are children, little boys and girls under the age of 15.

His domestic policies, whose viciousness is peewee in comparison with what he is so eager to do to foreigners who don't look like him and talk like him, who don't have names like his, nonetheless inflict pain on those Americans of the sort enumerated in the Beatitudes, by depriving them of decent health care and education, and of food, shelter and clothing when times are bad. It seems quite possible that his opinion of the American people has been formed while watching the Jerry Springer Show, which is Republican propaganda of the most pernicious kind.

But America was certainly hated all around the world long before this *coup d'état*. And we weren't hated, as George W. Bush would have it, because of our liberty and justice for all. We are hated because our corporations have been the principal deliverers and imposers of new technologies and economic schemes that have wrecked the self-respect, the cultures of men, women and children in so many other societies.

It's that simple. What are we to do when confronted by such hatred? Respond to Code Red and run around like chickens with their heads cut off.

Keep in touch,

Kurt Vonnegut

Written in the Night

The pain of living in the present world

John Berger

John Berger, the writer and critic, is the author of The Success and Failure of Piccaso *and* Art and Revolution. *He has written a number of novels, including* A Painter of our Time, Corker's Freedom, *and* 'G', *and is famous for his books of reportage,* A Fortunate Man, Ways of Seeing *and* A Seventh Man.

I want to say at least something about the pain existing in the world today. Consumerist ideology, which has become the most powerful and invasive on the planet, sets out to persuade us that pain is an accident, something that we can insure against. This is the logical basis for the ideology's pitilessness.

Everyone knows, of course, that pain is endemic to life, and wants to forget this or relativise it. All the variants of the myth of a Fall from the Golden Age, before pain existed, are an attempt to relativise the pain suffered on earth. So too is the invention of Hell, the adjacent kingdom of pain-as-punishment. Likewise the discovery of Sacrifice. And later, much later, the principle of Forgiveness. One could argue that philosophy began with the question: why pain?

Yet, when all this has been said, the present pain of living in the world is perhaps in some ways unprecedented.

I write in the night, although it is daytime. A day in early October 2002. For almost a week the sky above Paris has been blue. Each day the sunset is a little earlier and each day gloriously beautiful. Many fear that before the end of the month, US military forces will be launching the 'preventive' war against Iraq, so that the US oil corporations can lay their hands on further and supposedly safer oil supplies. Others hope that this can be avoided. Between the announced decisions and the secret calculations, everything is kept unclear, since lies prepare the way for missiles. I write in a night of shame. By shame I do not mean individual guilt. Shame, as I'm coming to understand it, is a species feeling which, in the long run, corrodes the capacity for hope and prevents us looking far ahead. We look down at our feet, thinking only of the next small step.

People everywhere, under very different conditions, are asking themselves – where are we? The question is historical not geographical. What are we living through? Where are we being taken? What have we lost? How to continue without a plausible vision of the future? Why have we lost any view of what is beyond a lifetime?

The well-heeled experts answer. Globalisation. Postmodernism. Communications revolution. Economic liberalism. The terms are tautological and evasive. To the anguished question of where are we, the experts murmur: nowhere. Might it not be better to see and declare that we are living through the most tyrannical – because the most pervasive – chaos that has ever existed? It's not easy to grasp the nature of the tyranny for its power structure (ranging from the 200 largest multinational corporations to the Pentagon) is interlocking yet diffuse, dictatorial yet anonymous, ubiquitous yet placeless. It tyrannises from off shore – not only in terms of fiscal law, but in terms of any political control beyond its own. Its aim is to delocalise the entire world. Its ideological strategy, besides which Osama bin Laden's is a fairy tale, is to undermine the existent so that everything collapses into its special version of the virtual, from the realm of which (and this is the tyranny's credo) there will be a never-ending source of profit. It sounds stupid. Tyrannies are stupid. This one is destroying at every level the life of the planet on which it operates.

Ideology apart, its power is based on two threats. The first is intervention from the sky by the most heavily armed state in the world. One could call it Threat B52. The second is of ruthless indebtment, bankruptcy, and hence, given the present productive relations in the world, starvation. One could call it Threat Zero.

The shame begins with the contestation (which we all acknowledge somewhere but, out of powerlessness, dismiss) that much of the present suffering could be alleviated or avoided if certain realistic and relatively simple decisions were taken. There is a very direct relation today between the minutes of meetings and minutes of agony.

Does anyone deserve to be condemned to certain death simply because they don't have access to treatment which would cost less than $2 a day? This was a question posed by the director of the World Health Organisation last July. She was talking about the Aids epidemic in Africa and elsewhere from which an estimated 68 million people will die within the next 18 years.

I'm talking about the pain of living in the present world.

Most analyses and prognoses about what is happening are understandably presented and studied within the framework of their separate disciplines: economics, politics, media studies, public health, ecology, national defence, criminology, education. In reality each of these separate fields is joined to another to make up the real terrain of what is being lived. It happens that in their lives people suffer from wrongs which are classified in separate categories, and suffer them simultaneously and inseparably.

A current example: some Kurds, who fled last week to Cherbourg, have been refused asylum by the French government and risk being repatriated to Turkey, are poor, politically undesirable, landless, exhausted, illegal and the clients of nobody. And they suffer each of these conditions at one and the same second. To take in what is happening, an interdisciplinary vision is necessary in order to connect the 'fields' which are institutionally kept separate. And any such vision is bound to be (in the original sense of the word) political. The precondition for thinking politically on a global scale is to see the unity of the unnecessary suffering taking place. This is the starting point.

I write in the night, but I see not only the tyranny. If that were so, I would probably not have the courage to continue. I see people sleeping, stirring, getting up to drink water, whispering their projects or their fears, making love, praying, cooking something whilst the rest of the family is asleep, in Baghdad and Chicago. (Yes, I see too the forever invincible Kurds, 4,000 of whom were gassed, with US compliance, by Saddam Hussein.) I see pastrycooks working in Tehran and the shepherds, thought of as bandits, sleeping beside their sheep in Sardinia, I see a man in the Friedrichshain quarter of Berlin sitting in his pyjamas with a bottle of beer reading Heidegger, and he has the hands of a proletarian, I see a small boat of illegal immigrants off the Spanish coast near Alicante, I see a mother in Mali – her name is Aya which means born on Friday – swaying her baby to sleep, I see the ruins of Kabul and a man going home, and I know that, despite the pain, the ingenuity of the survivors is undiminished, an ingenuity which scavenges and collects energy, and in the ceaseless cunning of this ingenuity, there is a spiritual value, something like the Holy Ghost. I am convinced of this in the night, although I don't know why.

The next step is to reject all the tyranny's discourse. Its terms are crap. In the interminably repetitive speeches, announcements, press conferences and threats, the recurrent terms are Democracy, Justice, Human Rights, Terrorism. Each word in the context signifies the opposite of what it was once meant to. Each has been trafficked, each has become a gang's code-word, stolen from humanity.

Democracy is a proposal (rarely realised) about decision-making; it has little to do with election campaigns. Its promise is that political decisions be made after, and in the light of, consultation with the governed. This is dependent upon the governed being adequately informed about the issues in question, and upon the decision-makers having the capacity and will to listen and take account of what they have heard. Democracy should not be confused with the 'freedom' of binary choices, the publication of opinion polls or the crowding of people into statistics. These are its pretence. Today the fundamental decisions, which effect the unnecessary pain increasingly suffered across the planet, have been and are taken unilaterally without any open consultation or participation. For instance, how many US citizens, if consulted, would have said specifically yes to Bush's withdrawal from the Kyoto agreement about the carbon dioxide greenhouse effect which is already provoking disastrous floods in many places, and threatens, within the next 25 years, far worse disasters? Despite all the media-managers of consent, I would suspect a minority.

It is a little more than a century ago that Dvořák composed his Symphony From the New World. He wrote it whilst directing a conservatory of music in New York, and the writing of it inspired him to compose, 18 months later, still in New York, his sublime Cello Concerto. In the symphony the horizons and rolling hills of his native Bohemia become the promises of the New World. Not grandiloquent but loud and continuing, for they correspond to the longings of those without power, of those who are wrongly called simple, of those the US Constitution addressed in 1787. I know of no other work of art which expresses so directly and yet so toughly (Dvořák was the son of a peasant and his father dreamt of his becoming a butcher) the beliefs which inspired generation after generation of migrants who became US citizens.

For Dvořák the force of these beliefs was inseparable from a kind of tenderness, a respect for life such as can be found intimately among the governed (as distinct from governors) everywhere. And it was in this spirit that the symphony was publicly received when it was first performed at Carnegie Hall (16 December 1893).

Dvořák was asked what he thought about the future of American music and he recommended that US composers listen to the music of the Indians and blacks. The Symphony From the New World expressed a hopefulness without frontiers which, paradoxically, is welcoming because centred on an idea of home. A utopian paradox.

Today the power of the same country which inspired such hopes has fallen into the hands of a coterie of fanatical (wanting to limit everything except the power of capital), ignorant (recognising only the reality of their own fire-power), hypocritical (two measures for all ethical judgments, one for us and another for them) and ruthless B52 plotters. How did this happen? How did Bush, Murdoch, Cheney, Kristol, Rumsfeld, *et al et* Arturo Ui, get where they did? The question is rhetorical, for there is no single answer, and it is idle, for no answer will dent their power yet. But to ask it in this way in the night reveals the enormity of what has happened. We are writing about the pain in the world.

The political mechanism of the new tyranny – although it needs highly sophisticated technology in order to function – is starkly simple. Usurp the words Democracy, Freedom, etc. Impose, whatever the disasters, the new profit-making and impoverishing economic chaos everywhere. Ensure that all frontiers are one-way: open to the tyranny, closed to others. And eliminate every opposition by calling it terrorist.

(No, I have not forgotten the couple who threw themselves from one of the Twin Towers instead of being burnt to death separately.)

There is a toy-like object which costs about $4 to manufacture and which is also incontestably terrorist. It is called the anti-personnel mine. Once launched, it is impossible to know who these mines will mutilate or kill, or when they will do so. There are more than 100 million lying on, or hidden in, the earth at this moment. The majority of victims have been or will be civilians.

The anti-personnel mine is meant to mutilate rather than kill. Its aim is to make cripples, and it is designed with shrapnel which, it is planned, will prolong the victim's medical treatment and render it more difficult. Most survivors have to undergo eight or nine surgical operations. Every month, as of now, 2,000 civilians somewhere are maimed or killed by these mines.

The description anti-personnel is linguistically murderous. Personnel are anonymous, nameless, without gender or age. Personnel is the opposite of people. As a term it ignores blood, limbs, pain, amputations, intimacy, and love. It abstracts totally. This is how its two words when joined to an explosive become terrorist.

The new tyranny, like other recent ones, depends to a large degree on a systematic abuse of language. Together we have to reclaim our hijacked words and reject the tyranny's nefarious euphemisms; if we do not, we will be left with only the word shame. Not a simple task, for most of its official discourse is pictorial, associative, evasive, full of innuendoes. Few things are said in black and white. Both military and economic strategists now realise that the media play a crucial role, not so much in defeating the current enemy as in foreclosing and preventing mutiny, protests or desertion.

Any tyranny's manipulation of the media is an index of its fears. The present one lives in fear of the world's desperation. A fear so deep that the adjective desperate, except when it means dangerous, is never used. Without money each daily human need becomes a pain.

Those who have filched power – and they are not all in office, so they reckon on a continuity of that power beyond presidential elections – pretend to be saving the world and offering its population the chance to become their clients. The world consumer is sacred. What they don't add is that consumers only matter because they generate profit, which is the only thing that is really sacred. This sleight of hand leads us to the crux. The claim to be saving the world masks the plotter's assumption that a large part of the world, including most of the continent of Africa and a considerable part of South America, is irredeemable. In fact, every corner which cannot be part of their centre is irredeemable. And such a conclusion follows inevitably from the dogma that the only salvation is money, and the only global future is the one their priorities insist upon, priorities which, with false names given to them, are in reality nothing more nor less than their benefits.

Those who have different visions or hopes for the world, along with those who cannot buy and who survive from day to day (approximately 800 million) are backward relics from another age, or, when they resist, either peacefully or with arms, terrorists. They are feared as harbingers of death, carriers of disease or insurrection. When they have been 'downsized' (one of the key words), the tyranny, in its naïveté, assumes the world will be unified. It needs its fantasy of a happy ending. A fantasy which in reality will be its undoing. Every form of contestation against this tyranny is comprehensible. Dialogue with it, impossible. For us to live and die properly, things have to be named properly. Let us reclaim our words

This is written in the night. In war the dark is on nobody's side, in love the dark confirms that we are together.

© Copyright John Berger

Pax Americana Fata Morgana!

Edy Korthals Altes

The first Dialogue on Peace and Human Rights in Europe and the Middle East took place in Cordoba in November (see Spokesman 77). It was jointly sponsored by the Russell Foundation and the City of Cordoba. Continuing with the publication of contributions to the Dialogue, we feature two more pieces, one from Europe and one from the Middle East (by Bahey el din Hassan).

Edy Korthals Altes is former Ambassador of The Netherlands and Honorary President of the World Conference of Religions and Peace.

The document on the National Security Strategy of the United States of America, presented to Congress by President George W. Bush, constitutes a radical break with the post-war efforts to build a world order on the basis of the United Nations. In blunt language, with little consideration for the sensitivity of other nations – even of those with a long and proud history – the document lays down the claims of the United States for world hegemony, based on unparalleled military strength and great economic/political influence. From now on, the United States – and the United States alone! – aspires to lead the world on the path of peace, freedom, democracy, development, free markets and free trade. The United Nations is relegated to a marginal role.

American leadership will prevail, if necessary, with the use of military power. The National Security Strategy shows no velvet on an iron fist. In a sense it codifies the manifest tendency towards unilateralism over the past few years: repudiation of the Anti-Ballistic Missile Treaty, rejection of the Kyoto Protocol, dropping out of the global effort to strengthen the bio-war Treaty, refusal to accept the International Criminal Court, the aggressive pursuit of the militarisation of space, and an unprecedented level of military expenditures. The heinous attacks on 9/11, together with the fear of use of weapons of mass destruction by 'rogue states', are given as the main reasons for the new Security Strategy. Of course, nobody will deny that these threats have to be taken seriously. But is the way the United States now intends to deal with them really the best way, or could this be counterproductive and even lead to much greater problems?

Furthermore, are these the only motives for the now proposed aggressive approach to world affairs? The military build-up has been going on for several years. And in the important document of the United States Space Command, *Vision 2020*, it is clearly spelt out that Full Spectrum Dominance is the objective, in order to protect American interests and investments. Neo-conservative groups, concerned about the possibility of maintaining the American way of life in a turbulent world in which the gap between rich and poor is widening, launched the Project for a New American Century. Their Report was already drawn up in 2000 by Dick Cheney, Ronald Rumsfeld and others. It envisages a global *Pax Americana* in order to safeguard national security and economic interests (oil!). It advocates an aggressive grand strategy, based on a military posture which it would be impossible to challenge.

The new National Security Strategy not only undermines the United Nations but also constitutes a threat to world peace. Loyal allies should therefore speak out frankly and not hide their misgivings for fear of hurting big brother. This applies in particular to Europe, which owes so much to the great American nation, which came twice to its rescue during two world wars. Genuine solidarity, however, does not imply a meek endorsement of a line of action which will lead to a destabilisation of international relations and an inadequate approach to pressing world problems. But critical observations should be accompanied by suggestions of a more promising, multilateral approach. It is in this constructive spirit that the following analysis of some of the main points is made.

The security situation

The post Cold War period indeed poses new threats. These are, however, not limited to Terrorism and Weapons of Mass Destruction (WMD), to which so much attention is given in the document. There are many other formidable threats to human security such as poverty, underdevelopment and the progressive destruction of our natural environment. What does security mean to well over a billion people who now suffer from poverty, hunger, disease, and the lack of basic health and educational facilities?

The present accent on military means is not only morally repugnant but also ignores the interconnectedness of the various threats to human security. It is a fatal illusion to think that security nowadays can be assured by the present emphasis on armed forces. The world has changed since the terrible events of 9/11. Unfortunately, political thinking still lags behind and fails to recognise three closely inter-linked and basic facts:
- the extreme vulnerability of modern society
- the apocalyptic destructive potential of modern arms and terrorist actions
- the interdependence in a global world, obliging us to practise justice and solidarity.

Confronting the manifold world-wide challenges to security requires a new approach, implying a basic correction of the momentous imbalance in the allocation of scarce resources.

The struggle against terrorism and the threat of weapons of mass destruction

At present, the emphasis is put on military means. Of course, there is a need for special security measures as well as a limited use of military means – within an international context – to eliminate terrorist networks. But great care should be taken to avoid actions which could be counterproductive; yes, even increasing the number of terrorists! In dealing with the complex phenomenon of terrorism, a wide range of measures will be necessary. Serious attention should be given to addressing the causes of terrorism. The document, however, is rather reluctant to touch on this aspect. It limits itself to the observation that poverty does not make poor people into terrorists, although it recognises that poverty, weak institutions and corruption can make weak states vulnerable to terrorists networks. It is significant that even a hardliner like Brzezinski is pleading to focus on the political roots of terrorism.

Competing for peace

President Bush, in his accompanying letter to the National Security Strategy, announces a new approach in international affairs. He rightly sees an historic opportunity to build a world where great powers compete in peace, instead of continually preparing for war. But, frankly speaking, is this not rather a cynical statement of the President of a nation which has not only succeeded in building up a military potential of grotesque proportions – capable of fighting several major wars at the same time – but also continues to invest vast resources in a further build up? How can one talk about 'competing for peace' with well over $400 billion in military expenditure and only about $10 billion for official development aid? Even the proposed 50 per cent increase of this minimal amount will not alter much the perception that the United States – with its 0.1 per cent of gross national product for overseas development aid – is lagging way behind the United Nations objective of 0.7 per cent!

Indeed, a new approach towards global security, an effective competition for peace, is urgently needed. This should not only involve a drastic reshuffling of resources, but also lead to a revision of trade, agricultural and fishery policies affecting nations in the process of development. 'Competing for peace' should imply a critical reappraisal of our approach towards the problem of poverty and underdevelopment and a preparedness to adjust policies, whenever the legitimate interests of the poorer nations are harmed. This should also bring to an end the hypocrisy of many developed nations who, insisting on open markets from developing countries, keep their own markets closed to products from developing nations.

Pre-emption and counter-proliferation

The readiness to resort to military violence in confronting the threats of terrorism and rogue states gives rise to great concern. In particular, there is the notion that the United States is prepared to impose its will through the use of military power, whenever this is considered to be necessary for defence or the protection of its interests. President Chirac has rightly drawn attention to the dangerous consequences of this approach. Indeed, if one nation sets the example, others will be tempted to follow, claiming a similar right to interfere. Instead of reinforcing the international security regime, we risk falling back into an international jungle.

The statement that deterrence and containment are no longer adequate to deal with the new security threat may apply to terrorists, but even a rogue state will think twice before considering an attack on a superpower.

A coalition among the great powers

The National Security Strategy acknowledges 'There is little of lasting consequence that the USA can accomplish in the world without the sustained co-operation of its allies and friends in Canada and Europe'. This, however, will not be facilitated by the imposition of American policies provoking irritation and frustrations. It also remains to be seen whether 'coalition building' with Russia, China and India has been made easier after this analysis of their achievements and differences, telling them – from a superior position – what remains to be done. Indicative of the proposed way of functioning of this coalition is the phrase 'consultations yes, but we will not hesitate to act alone if we consider this necessary'. The same resolve we find in Secretary of Defence Rumsfeld's statement 'The mission determines the coalition, we don't allow coalitions to determine the mission'.

Repeatedly mention is made in the document of the need to establish a balance of power in support of freedom. But how should this be realised when it is made clear from the outset that the United States does not allow any challenge to American leadership? No other powers will be permitted to match them. 'Our forces will be strong enough to dissuade potential adversaries from pursuing a military build-up in hopes of surpassing, or equalling, the power of the United States.'

'Balance of power' was a popular notion in bygone centuries. It has led to many bloody wars. With the founding of the United Nations it was hoped to create a different international order, offering a better perspective for peace and justice.

The role of Nato

Although the core mission – collective defence of the transatlantic alliance – remains, it becomes clear from the National Security Strategy that Nato's relevance for the United States depends on the development of new structures and capabilities enabling it to carry out 'appropriate combat contributions in coalition warfare', wherever necessary. The future of Nato clearly depends on meeting a whole list of requirements, among them the pressing demand for a substantial increase of defence budgets! 'If Nato succeeds in enacting these changes, the rewards will be a partnership as central to the security and interests of its member states as was the case during the Cold War.'

The reorientation and enlargement of Nato will be decided during the summit meeting in Prague, at the end of November 2002. Here, emphasis will be placed on its military character, in particular the capabilities/preparedness to operate anywhere in the world. But do the European partners realise that the proposed Nato intervention force implies the full political responsibility for these actions, even if their active contribution may be rather modest? Certainly, the transatlantic partnership is very important, but not at any price! Differences between the United States and European nations do exist, not only in the appreciation of the international situation but also in the economic field. Is it really in the European interest to move from a collective defence organisation towards an instrument in the hands of the United States for military interventions elsewhere in the world, particularly in a set-up in which the possibilities to influence the decision-making process are rather limited?

Of crucial importance for the future of the Atlantic Alliance would be a common deliberation in Prague about the present concept of security. Excessive attention is still given to building up a position of military strength, assuming that this is the best way to safeguard national interests. This, however, ignores the substantial threats to security posed by pressing world problems requiring non-military means. Means which will never become available without a drastic revision of priorities in spending as world-wide military spending stands in no comparison with the means available for addressing urgent world problems. The imbalance is striking!

Freedom

Freedom is – as President Bush rightly states – indeed a great achievement and an essential element for human development. It should, however, always be embedded in an ethical context. What is urgently needed, therefore, at this critical moment, is a creative dialogue on the common path towards a just and peaceful world order. An order based on humane values such as respect for life, justice, tolerance, solidarity and compassion. This should now be the common challenge, not only for governments but also for citizens, non-governmental organisations and religions, both in the United States of America and Europe.

Conclusion

In the National Security Strategy, two lines come together. A deep sense of insecurity, yes even genuine fear, is meeting with a strong awareness of unprecedented power. It has resulted in placing exclusive trust in American strength, not in the United Nations. If this world is going to survive, a far greater imaginative effort has to be made to create the conditions for peace. The challenge of President Bush to 'compete for peace' has to be taken up. This should not, however, lead to a greater reliance upon the unilateral use of military means, but to a far greater common effort to address major world problems, involving a radical reallocation of scarce resources.

A structural reform of the United Nations is also urgently needed, in order to bring this Organisation in to line with the profound changes which have taken place since its founding. Our world is in dire need of strong and efficient global and regional institutions.

Unilateralism – now presented as American Internationalism – is bound to lead to deep irritation, yes, stubborn resistance, even from traditional allies. Although the United States, with its overwhelming military power, is capable of eradicating every nation on this planet, it should realise that security can only be obtained on the basis of a just and sustainable world order. Trying to keep control of the world while striving to maintain a morally and politically unacceptable social and economic situation, will inevitably lead to a fatal explosion. Unilateral imperial leadership, in our highly interdependent world, is an anachronism!

The proclaimed *Pax Americana* will not enhance security, but instead endanger world stability. It will be fraught with a great deal of turmoil and suffering. It will prove to be a *fata Morgana!*

Don't attack IRAQ

Let's have a war on POVERTY

John Cogger
president

Bob Crow
general secretary

'War on Terrorism' – War against Human Rights

Bahey el din Hassan

The author, Director of the Cairo Institute For Human Rights Studies, read this paper at the Cordoba seminar.

There is almost a consensus amongst analysts of terrorism world-wide that it is the outcome of many interwoven factors – political, economic, social and cultural. Their analyses have not changed much since September 11, 2001, despite the intense light shone on the Islamic background of the Al Qaeda group accused of planning and perpetrating these attacks.

This explanation of the growth of terrorism can be summarised as follows: 'the North's marginalisation of the South; the growing neglect of the poor and underdeveloped countries; the North's short-sighted and misguided emphasis on economic rather than political forces in determining the development of the world; the expanding gap between power and the rule of international law, and a keenness on the part of some Northern states to exploit this gap in furthering their interests across the globe; the sharp contradiction in the North's foreign policy with respect to Palestinian rights, especially the United States' blind support of Israel; the support of some corrupt and despotic regimes in the pursuit of self-interest, profit and geopolitical power, and the undermining of economic, social and political human rights in the South.'*

Such an understanding of terrorism cannot be traced in the conduct of the current 'War on Terrorism', which is dominated by its security and military character clearly embodied in the United Nations Security Council resolution no. 1373 of September 28, 2001. This totally neglected the strategic tasks which are highly relevant to the political, social and cultural environment in which terrorism incubates.

At an early stage, many observers and analysts expressed their concern about how the 'international campaign against Terrorism' was

---

*The Final Report of the International Conference on 'Terrorism and Human Rights' January 2002. Cairo Institute For Human Rights.

being managed. They were particularly concerned about the solo management of the campaign by the United States, and the marginalising of the role of the United Nation, as well as the use of almost exclusively military means whilst ignoring the interrelation between security and respect for human rights. Further cause for concern was given by other states using this climate to strengthen their control over minorities or peoples subject to their occupation. This is what really happened in Palestine and Chechnya. It aggravates, rather than impedes, terrorism because the 'War on Terrorism' itself nourishes the soil incubating terrorism. This process is represented in the following ways .

Firstly, the 'War on Terrorism' exhibits disregard for and irresponsibility towards international law and the institutions of the international community. This represents an incitement to all parties – groups, peoples and states – to resort to violence for resolution of conflicts and the attainment of rights. In turn, this further marginalises the institutions of the international community and degrades the moral and political status of international law. This disdain reached its utmost in the position of the United States with respect to the International Criminal Court (ICC), when it withdrew its signature to the convention establishing the Court and urged other states to do likewise. Furthermore, the United States has concluded bilateral agreements – based on blackmail – with other states to protect American soldiers from prosecution by the International Criminal Court. A draft bill has been submitted to Congress that would allow the United States to undertake military operations to release American soldiers who may be detained pending trial in The Hague. This bill is known as the 'Netherlands Invasion Bill'!!!

Secondly, the 'War on Terrorism' explicitly violates human rights world-wide, both in practice and legislatively, including both Europe and the United States. Laws have been enacted that severely circumvent freedoms and civil rights, including the rights of political asylum-seekers and migrants. Several Third World and Arab countries have followed suit, enacting more restrictive legislation and claiming as justification similar acts by countries of the North. Advocates of democracy and human rights have been harassed and arrested, and many of them have been subjected to unfair trials. It is most unfortunate that the hysterical climate created by the September 11 attacks has made the 'War on Terrorism' an actual war on human rights.

Human rights considerations were set aside. Rules of international humanitarian law were blatantly violated during the war launched by the United States in Afghanistan in the name of the international coalition against terrorism, in co-operation with the Afghan armed factions opposing the Taliban regime. It has become difficult to discern between states with major democratic traditions and third world authoritarian regimes in the contest for restricting civil freedoms, undermining human rights guarantees and privacy, and adopting exceptional measures that threaten the rights of minorities and asylum-seekers in the name of security, stability and combating terrorism. When human rights are undermined in democratic states of international weight, such as the United States, which are supposed to be followed as examples, it amounts to giving a free hand to dictatorships and authoritarian regimes in the world to violate human rights without being held accountable.

Thirdly, the 'War on Terrorism' exacerbates the 'Clash of Civilizations' scenario, and thus revives racial hatred against Arabs and Muslims in particular. Thus, since September 11, the political climate has aggravated racist tendencies towards Arabs and Muslims in Europe and North America, and allowed the spread of racist ideas closely related to the clash of civilizations and the discourse of mutual hatred between the West on the one hand and Arabs and Muslims on the other. Moreover, these racist ideas have become an ideological cover which is used by both parties to mobilise the forces of extremism, fanaticism and hatred of the other. This portends the undermining of the creative, global efforts to combat terrorism and ensure the most suitable conditions for cultural coexistence in a context of respect for cultural diversity and the right of different cultures to equal self-expression.

Fourthly, the 'War on Terrorism' aggravates feelings of injustice, shunning fairness and impartial solutions based on the principles of the right to self-determination, justice, equality and equity. Palestine is the most prominent example, where the Israeli occupation has been condoned and justified. The massacres committed during the last year have been allegedly advocated as a 'War on Terrorism', and as legitimate self-defence. Other examples include Chechnya, Kashmir and Iraq, which became the next victim of the so-called 'War on Terrorism'.

Bin Laden attempted to use the defence of the rights of the Palestinian people as a pretext to justify the September 11 crime and to endow it with legitimacy. However, the Israeli terrorist state of racist settler occupation was more successful in making use of September 11. It succeeded in portraying the legitimate right of the Palestinian people to resist the occupation and to self-defence against Israel's continued oppression, given the failure of international mechanisms to support it with assistance and protection, as a kind of terrorism that Israel has to deal with in the same way that terrorism was dealt with in Afghanistan

Paradoxically, the United States did not wait more than 26 days before it launched a war in response to the September 11 attacks, whereas it vents its wrath upon the Palestinian people for not enduring 34 years of Israeli occupation and terrorism and 53 years of oppression, massacres and expulsions. Even worse, the United States gave Sharon, the war criminal, a green light to proceed with shedding the blood of the Palestinians. Meanwhile, it continues to impede any possible international mechanism for protecting the Palestinian people through its influence in the United Nations Security Council.

Throughout the past two years, the Palestinian people has been subjected to a brutal war in which the Israeli military have used Apache helicopters, F16 aircraft, tanks, armoured vehicles, and even naval artillery. The number of murdered Palestinians has reached 1,800, 20 per cent of them children. This is in addition to 7,000 injured children, 500 of whom are deformed for life.

In fact, life in Gaza and the West Bank has been totally paralysed. Gaza is totally isolated from the rest of Palestine. All the cities and villages of the West Bank are dispersed, and checkpoints have been established at all their entrances. The Palestinian economy has collapsed. Average individual income has decreased to US$ 2 per month. More Palestinian agricultural lands have been swept away, particularly in Gaza. Gross national income has decreased by 60 per cent. Unemployment has increased to 50 per cent in the cities and 85 per cent in rural areas. Seventy per cent of the Palestinian people now live below the poverty line.

From moral, philosophical and practical perspectives, it has become difficult to distinguish between the discourse of terrorism as represented by Bin Laden's discourse, and the discourse of the 'War on Terrorism' represented in the discourse of the American administration. Both discourses are based on one orthodox and extremist philosophy which believes that the end justifies the means, and that the only means, regardless of their legitimacy, are force and violence. Both discourses are almost identical in their disdain of the philosophy of law, of international law, and of the institutions of the international community. They either refuse to recognise them theoretically (as in Bin Laden's case), or marginalise and dominate them (as the United States does).

Both discourses believe that the world is a jungle in which sovereignty is for the stronger. Thus the rule of law for both of them means nothing but their own laws, i.e. the rule of force.

Why Chernobyl Still Matters

Rosalie Bertell

Dr Bertell is President Emerita of the International Institute of Concern for Public Health and Member of the Board of Regents, International Association of Humanitarian Medicine. Her most recent book is Planet Earth: The Latest Weapon of War (The Women's Press).

Journalists and mathematicians have a way of focusing on one aspect of a complex situation in order to give a snapshot view of its magnitude. For example, one might read in the newspaper that a 'six alarm fire' had occurred in some neighbourhood. This immediately conjures up the image of a very large fire requiring six fire stations to send trucks to the scene. It gives one no clue as to the magnitude of loss of life or property, the water or smoke damage, the impact on human lives and health, ecological impact, and so on. Another example is that of a television show rating scale. If you see an estimate of five million viewers of some special event television, you immediately understand that this is a 'rounded number' meant for comparison only, which does not reveal how many people actually watched the show. Certainly some televisions played to an empty room and some to a large number of people watching the display in the local pub. It gives no indication of whether the watchers reacted positively or negatively to the programme. If the event is important, we expect professionals to fill in the details later.

Another misleading human custom is presenting an event as 'small' when there exist more traumatic forms of the event. For example, the radiation exposure to depleted uranium in the Gulf War is presented as 'small' in the face of a nuclear holocaust. Such exposure is not 'small' for the victims.

Unfortunately, many government officials, physicists, and engineers have used this tactic to deliberately minimise the health effects of radiation, and in particular the immense suffering after the 1986 Chernobyl disaster. For example, some people actually believe that the magnitude of a nuclear accident can be gauged by the potential number of cancer deaths it will cause, and further, that cancer death is the only consequence! Minimalist reporting occurred after the Three Mile Island accident, downwind of nuclear weapon testing, and at serious military accidents like the one which spread plutonium in farmland in Spain. Most recently it has attempted to deny that exposure to depleted uranium weapons has caused severe health damage to the military veterans and the civilians in Iraq, Kosovo and, most likely, in Afghanistan.

The minimalist reporting went even further with Chernobyl. The IAEA (International Atomic Energy Agency) and UNSCEAR (United Nations Scientific Committee on Atomic Radiation) recent statement that 'only 32 deaths occurred, 200 were heavily irradiated and 2000 avoidable thyroid cancers' resulted from the Chernobyl disaster goes well beyond a mathematical short hand which gives an immediate sketch about a disaster. This fifteen-years-later report about a complex, painful situation should be much more precise and believable! It rather tries to obliterate from people's minds and concerns the suffering of millions of persons in rural and un-evacuated areas who were exposed, and hundreds of thousands evacuated but not medically examined victims. When one probes a little more deeply, one finds that the honest scientists and physicians, trying to explain the widespread injuries and long term effects of nuclear exposure, have been silenced.

In fact immediately after the disaster of April 26, 1986, due to International Atomic Energy Agency policy, unless a person had been declared 'overexposed' at the medical tent set up for the 'liquidators' of the disaster, he or she was officially considered to be a 'radio-phobia' case, a purely psychological phenomenon. Local physicians told people that there would be no medical effects of exposure until, perhaps in ten or twenty years, they may happen to develop cancer. But, not to worry! These future radio-genic cancers would be indistinguishable from 'natural' cancers. The physicians soon learned from direct evidence of pathological injuries that this information from the physicists was less than candid. It was not surprising to learn that those who tried to minimise the disaster were the same people charged with promoting nuclear industries, for example, marketing nuclear reactors to the developing nations.

The experience of Chernobyl is not unique, but follows the secrecy pattern used at many lesser accidents which were mishandled in the same way. This has occurred both in the developed and developing world. In particular, I would note the radioactive pollution of the Mitsubishi Asian Rare Earth facility in Bukit Merah, Malaysia, the radioactive waste dumped in Nigeria, and the contaminated food distributed to Egypt, Papua New Guinea, India and other countries during the Chernobyl disaster clean-up.

However, the health problems due to Chernobyl continue to be very acute right now, and demand international attention and action. Scientists and physicians are deprived of their freedom, and the people, especially the children, are suffering. This crisis can serve to point out the serious secrecy, vested interest and collusion of international agencies protecting nuclear technologies. The public face of the nuclear industry has been 'clean and safe'. It is important to unmask this public face, serving as a warning to economically developing countries deciding on energy technologies and bringing needed humanitarian aid to the victims. Preserving the false image of nuclear technology keeps the industry and nuclear agencies in business.

Lessons from Hiroshima and Nagasaki

Unlike the general study of toxic materials, handled by toxicologists, the field of radiation and health has been dominated by physicists, engineers and mathematicians since the dawn of the nuclear era in 1943. Their health related communications differ radically in content from similar communications of health professionals in Toxicology, Occupational or Public Health.

This field of radiation health was, with a few exceptions, taken over by the physicists of the Manhattan Project after World War Two, in their effort to contain the secrets of the nuclear age. Radiation was an effect of the atomic bomb. Secrecy caused these 'hard scientists' to fail to consider the broad range of responses and varieties of vulnerabilities possessed by a living population exposed to this hazard. Such variation in biological responses would have been expected by health professionals.

Because of Hiroshima and Nagasaki, most people now know about acute radiation exposure syndrome, with vomiting, hair falling out, alterations in blood cells, and so on, and this bit of information has been translated into a naïve belief on the part of the public, that unless acute radiation sickness has been documented (often by the government physicists) any subsequent severe illness observed in radiation exposed persons is due to something, anything, but not radiation exposure. This has some historical validity, but at Chernobyl with millions of exposed persons in rural un-evacuated areas, hundreds of thousands evacuated but not medically examined, and with the population's continuous ingestion of contaminated foods for the past fifteen years, demanding documentation of radiation sickness is ridiculous. Even in the Japanese cities radiation sickness went undocumented for many victims. Radiation injury is not predicated on documentation of acute radiation sickness, but rather on the alteration of a cell leading to a fatal cancer. It is well documented the these cellular level events can occur well below the level of exposure which causes overt sickness. The amount of energy released by just one nuclear transformation of one atom of a radioactive material is measured in thousands or millions of electron volts. It requires only 6 to 10 electron volts to break the molecular bounds in the cellular DNA and RNA which carry the genes for life.

In Hiroshima and Nagasaki (1945), exposure and subsequent health records were not complete. The research stations did not begin to select a study population until after the 1950 Japanese census identified survivors and a 1967 dose estimate was derived by the scientists at Oak Ridge National Laboratory in the United States. Deaths prior to 1950 were ignored. Death certificates, which were at times incomplete, were used to determine first cause of death of the study population. Cancers which were not fatal were not reported until 1994. Most survivors are still alive so their 'cause of death' has not yet been studied. Other non-cancer health problems were considered to be 'not of concern' and have not been systematically reported.

There were persons who entered the contaminated territories of Hiroshima and Nagasaki after the fire died down, or who consumed radioactive contaminated food and water, who experienced radiation sickness, but were not officially recognised as 'exposed'. They are in the radiation exposure control group. This is easily explained to the mathematician, who is told that the Hiroshima and Nagasaki studies looked for the effects of the immediate penetrating radiation from the exploding bomb on the persons who were within three kilometres of the hypocentre at that moment. For the military person looking for information on the health effects of radiation due to the bomb, this artificial limitation made some sense. However, if a civil society is seeking information on the effects of man-made radiation on the human body, then all sources of that man-made radiation, including that from nuclear fall-out, food and water contamination, residual radioactive debris at the bomb site, and so on, is important. Changing the definition of 'exposed to man-made radiation' to mean 'exposed to the bomb', and then using this research to back public and occupational health policy is problematic to say the least!

Because of this concentration on the first flash of the atomic bomb, serious mistakes have been made by the radiation physicists in estimating the biological damage done by ingested or inhaled radioactive particles, many of which remain in the body for a long time and even enter into biochemical reactions of the cell's genetic material.

It is this atomic bomb study which appears to be dictating much of the inappropriate behaviour of officials with respect to the medical treatment of survivors of Chernobyl and other nuclear accidents. It has also caused harsh treatment of the honest scientists and physicians who spoke directly for the needs of the exposed suffering people. Many of these scientists and physicians, now in prison or effectively silenced, have conducted well designed and executed scientific studies.

Due to the complications generated by the study of external irradiation by a bomb being used to evaluate civilian exposures to inhaled or ingested radioactivity, and the use of this research to educate young physicists and nuclear engineers, many scientific blunders and administrative problems were generated. The failure to deal with the whole breadth of radiation problems became entrenched in the very agencies which were created in the 1950s to protect the public at risk from atmospheric nuclear testing. I will try to unravel the problems with the International Atomic Energy Agency (IAEA), the United Nations Scientific Committee on Atomic Radiation (UNSCEAR), the International Commission on Radiological Protection (ICRP), the US National Academy of Science Biological Effects of Ionising Radiation Committee (BEIR) and the World Health Organisation(WHO). All of these organisations, except the World Health Organisation, which was relegated to treating the victims rather than understanding the problem, play key parts with respect to current radiation and public health policies and understandings. Ironically, the World Health Organisation, created by the United Nations in 1948, was not given any role in the health assessment of this global threat to human and ecological health.

United Nations Initiatives

Nuclear bombs were first used in war in 1945, when the United States used them against Japan in Hiroshima and Nagasaki. As early as 1946, the United States began atmospheric testing of nuclear bombs in the Marshall Islands, in the Pacific Ocean. The former Soviet Union demonstrated that it had the nuclear bomb in 1949, and there was tangible fear of a nuclear exchange during the Korean War. The United Kingdom began nuclear weapon testing off the coast of Australia in the 1950s, and then on the continent itself and in the Pacific Islands.

The first atomic bombs were based on fission, and because of this they were limited in their destructive power. The force of the explosion blew apart the fissioning materials, terminating the explosive energy release. In 1954, the United States tested a thermonuclear device (hydrogen bomb), called Bravo, at Bikini Atoll in the Marshall Islands, demonstrating that a nuclear device with unlimited power could be built. This one was about one thousand times more powerful than the Hiroshima bomb. It was this military accomplishment which prompted the 'Peaceful Atom' speech of President Dwight Eisenhower before the United Nations, also in 1954.

The speech followed a shift in United States Military Policy to dependence on nuclear bombs and a rush towards production of uranium and the technology necessary to carry this out through a major weapon replacement programme: uranium mining and milling, uranium processing facilities, nuclear fuel fabrication facilities, nuclear production reactors, reprocessing facilities and the hazardous transportation and waste associated with each of these industries. In order to obtain American and global co-operation during peace time, there was a perceived need for commercial or so called 'peaceful uses' of nuclear technologies which would justify everyone's co-operation in the nation and the international community. Nuclear electrical production was billed as capable of fulfilling all of the energy needs of the developing world, and being 'too cheap to meter'. It was promoted as the hope of preventing future wars since no country would be in need!

In 1955, the United Nations responded by creating the United Nations Scientific Committee on Atomic Radiation (Res 913(X) 1955) to 'assess and report levels and effects of exposure to ionising radiation'. According to the UNSCEAR web site, 'governments and organisations throughout the world rely on the Committee's estimates as the scientific basis for evaluating radiation risk, establishing radiation protection and safety standards, and regulating radiation exposure.' UNSCEAR was envisioned as an organisation of physicists, who at that time were the only ones who could measure radiation since it escapes our senses and requires specialised instruments for detection. They were the experts on the hazard of ionising radiation, but failed to have the expertise to predict the varied human response to exposure to this hazard. In an odd way, perhaps because of their training in physics, they managed to average all exposures over the entire population of the world, now some six billion people. Natural background, because it is ubiquitous, rather homogeneously exposes everyone. However, a localised accident or relatively small workforce's exposure, when averaged over the whole population, can be made to seem trivial. It is not trivial to those who receive the exposure!

The United Nations Scientific Committee on Atomic Radiation became primarily a reporting agency, detailing the measurement of radioactive fallout, worker exposures and eventually emissions from nuclear power plants. I would assume that legislators saw this agency as providing independent monitoring of nuclear activities as a check on predicted pollution and theoretical estimates of harm. Unfortunately, UNSCEAR incorporated into its midst those same scientists who were making the predictions and estimating 'no harm from low level radiation'. No other industry is allowed to monitor itself. We do not ask the tobacco companies to tell us about tobacco's harm, or the pesticide companies to tell us the effects of their products on children. More on this point later.

In 1957, in response to Eisenhower's 'Peaceful Atom' speech, the United Nations also established the International Atomic Energy Agency, which describes itself as 'an independent intergovernmental, science and technology based organisation, in the United Nations family, that serves as the global focus point for nuclear co-operation.' Its mandate is described as: 'to promote peaceful uses of nuclear technology, develop safety standards, and verify that nuclear weapon technology did not spread horizontally to the non-nuclear Nations'. They had no mandate with respect to the nuclear weapons of the five nuclear states. Because of their nuclear watch-dog task, the International Atomic Energy Agency reports directly to the United Nations Security Council.

Response of the World Health Organisation

In 1957, the World Health Organisation, which was founded by the United Nations in 1948, became alarmed about the atmospheric nuclear testing and the proposed expansion of this technology for 'peaceful uses'. It called together eminent geneticists to consider the threat this exposure would pose to the human and ecological gene pool. Professor Hermann Muller, the geneticist who, in 1944, received a Nobel Prize for his work on genetic mutations of the fruit fly using ionising radiation, was a participant at this conference. Although the United States had not sent him as its delegate, he received a standing ovation at the conference for his work, and he consistently opposed the extension of nuclear technology into civilian uses. The conclusion of this expert group was that there was not enough information available in the scientific community to assure the integrity of future generations should the burden of ionising radiation exposure be increased. They called for extreme caution and further genetic investigations, especially in Kerala, India, where there is a high natural background level of radiation, and people have lived in this environment for hundreds of years. These recommendations were never implemented by governments anxious to get on with nuclear activities.

Later, an independent non-governmental organisation in India studied genetic damage in the high radiation background area and found it indeed significantly increased. An Article by B.A.Bridges in *Radiation Research* (Vol 156, 631-641; 2001) suggests that genetic mutations due to radiation imply that 'the nature of the radiation dose response cannot be assumed'. There is more complexity than was expected in the health consequences of changed DNA sequences. The serious implications of nuclear pollution for future generations is still an area of research demanding more than ordinary caution.

One can guess at the politics behind a second World Health Organisation conference of psychiatrists, called later in 1957 to consider the Public Health impact of peaceful nuclear activities. These professionals concluded that such activities could cause undue stress to the population because of the association with the atomic bomb. One finds that this has become a mantra for the physicists who have subsequently controlled all information relative to the health impact of nuclear technologies. Most recently, when the United Nations Scientific Committee on Atomic Radiation released its 15 year assessment of the Chernobyl disaster, one of its spokespersons, Dr. Neil Wald, Professor of Occupational and Environmental Health at the University of Pittsburgh School of Public Health, stated: 'It is important that public misperceptions be reduced as much as possible in this area, because unwarranted perception and fear of harm can itself produce avoidable health problems, as well as erroneous societal benefit versus risk judgements.' Loosely translated, Dr. Wald appears to be saying: 'if the public gets upset we will not be able to make our money with this nuclear technology'.

After the Three Mile Island accident in 1979, in response to the people's demand for a health study, the government organised a study headed by a psychiatrist from the Annapolis Naval Academy. He drew concentric circles around the failed nuclear reactor and compared the cancer rates and also the levels of fear and tension of those living within these layers. A sensible study would have looked down wind for air borne radionuclide effects, and down stream for the water-borne effects. This official study found only fear, which was positively correlated with distance from the plant.

There were about 2000 injury cases from the Three Mile Island population taken to court for compensation of health damage due to the radiation exposure. The nuclear company fought all the way to the United States Supreme Court against the courts even hearing these cases, and lost. Then the industry found an old law stating that an expert witness must use the methodology used by other professionals in their field, and using this, the nuclear company managed to disqualify every expert witness (physicians, epidemiologists, botanists, biologists) brought in by the victims. The physicists and engineers claimed sole expertise in the area of radiation health effects. All cases were dismissed by the court without one being heard.

A Deal Between the World Health Organisation and the International Atomic Energy Agency

This potential conflict between those who wished to exploit the new nuclear technology for both profit and military power, and the custodians of the public health, was superficially resolved by an Agreement (Res. WHA 12-40, 28 May 1959) stating that the International Atomic Energy Agency and the World Health Organisation recognise that ...'the IAEA has the primary responsibility for encouraging, assisting and co-ordinating research on, and development and practical applications of atomic energy for peaceful uses throughout the world without prejudice to the right of the WHO to concern itself with promoting, developing, assisting and co-ordinating international health work, including research, in all its aspects.' If the reader is confused, so is the writer. To understand this, one needs to know that the health effects of radiation were classified as secret under the United States Atomic Energy Act for national security. The 'international health work' assigned to the World Health Organisation was taking care of the victims. While technically the International Atomic Energy Agency and the World Health Organisation are 'equal' in the United Nations family, those agencies which report directly to the Security Council, as does the Agency, have more status.

In Article I (3) of the WHO/IAEA agreement, it is stated that 'Whenever either organisation proposes to initiate a programme or activity on a subject in which the other organisation has or may have a substantial interest, the first party shall consult with the other with a view to adjusting the matter by mutual consent'. This clause seems to have weakened the World Health Organisation from investigating the Chernobyl disaster, and gave the International Atomic Energy Agency a green light to bring in physicists and medical radiologists to assess the damage relative to their limited knowledge of the health effects of radiation. (Note: while radiologists use ionising radiation in their work, they deal with health damage only after the patient receives therapy levels of radiation.) This first evaluation used a different epidemiological protocol in each geographical area and with different age groups, eliminated all concern for cancers as not having sufficient latency periods and failed to note the extraordinary epidemic of thyroid diseases and cancers. From the point of view of Medical Epidemiology they failed miserably to deal with the reality. The director of this 1991 Epidemiological study, Dr. Fred Mettler, is a Medical Radiologist. There were no Epidemiologists, Public Health professionals or Toxicologists on the International Atomic Energy Agency Team.

The Self-Established International Commission on Radiological Protection

The United Nations Scientific Committee on Atomic Radiation has continued to be the measurement agency, which verifies that all planned releases of ionising radiation to the environment, and all exposures of workers, are 'acceptable'. It fell to the International Atomic Energy Agency to 'establish or adopt, in collaboration with other competent international bodies, standards of safety for the protection of health and to provide for the application of these standards'.

Neither the International Atomic Energy Agency nor the United Nations Scientific Committee on Atomic Radiation turned to the World Health Organisation to develop such protective health standards. Instead, they both turned to a self-appointed non-governmental organisation formed by the physicists of the Manhattan project together with the Medical Radiologists, who had organised themselves in 1928 to protect themselves and their colleagues from the severe consequences of exposure to medical X-ray. This new organisation, called the International Commission on Radiological Protection (ICRP), has a Main Committee of 13 persons who make all decisions. Members of this Main Committee were originally self-appointed, and have been perpetuated by being proposed by current members and accepted by the current executive committee. No outside agency can place a member on the International Commission on Radiological Protection, not even the World Health Organisation.

The United Nations Scientific Committee on Atomic Radiation 2000 Report was prepared by a Committee including the following seven persons who also serve on the thirteen person Main Committee of the International Commission on Radiological Protection: Prof. Roger Clark (currently the Chair of the International Commission), Prof. Rudolf M. Alexakhim, Dr. John D. Boice Jr., Prof. Fred A. Mettler Jr.(the same radiologist who headed the International Atomic Energy Agency Chernobyl epidemiological study), Dr. Zi Quiang Pan, and Dr. Yasuhito Sasaki.

It is the International Commission on Radiological Protection which makes recommendations for the protection of human health for workers and the general public. By their own admission, they are not a public or environmental health organisation. They have given themselves the task of recommending a trade-off of predictable health effects of exposure to radiation for the benefits of nuclear activities (including the production and testing of nuclear weapons). Their recommendations were first set in 1957, when the medical radiologists accepted the proposal which had been hammered out by the British, Canadian and American physicists after World War Two.

The original recommendation that workers be allowed 15 rad (150 mSv) per year was opposed by the British National Radiological Protection Board and an independent committee called the BEAR (Biological Effects of Atomic Radiation) funded in the United States by the Rockefeller Foundation. This forced the International Commission on Radiological Protection to reduce their recommendation for nuclear workers to 5 rad (50 mSv) per year. Maximum permissible doses for members of the public were ten times lower. This recommendation remained in effect until 1990, when under pressure from more than 700 scientists and physicians, and after a reassignment of doses at the atomic bomb research centres, the worker exposure was reduced to 2 rad (20 mSv) per year, while exposures to the public were reduced by another factor of five to 0.1 rad (1 mSv) per year.

Who Takes Responsibility?

It is important to note that no agency takes responsibility for these recommendations, and the World Health Organisation is excluded from professional collaboration or comment on them. The International Commission on Radiological Protection recommends, and the Nations are free to implement or not these recommendations. The Nations generally accept International Commission on Radiological Protection recommendations claiming that they do not have the expertise or money to derive their own standards. The recommendations are for a risk benefit trade off, and do not pretend to be based solely (or primarily) on protecting the public or worker health.

The International Atomic Energy Agency states: 'The underlying biological basis of the standards over the last several decades has rested primarily on the United Nations Scientific Committee on Atomic Radiation. This Committee was originally formed during the period of atmospheric weapon testing to assess the physical processes and health effects of fall out, but has since broadened its remit considerably'. UNSCEAR contains and depends on the leaders of the Main Committee of the International Commission on Radiological Protection. Those who set the standards also judge them to be adequate! Usually scientific theory is tested against reality and rejected if it fails to conform. Radiation health predictions are tested against the reality of the victims, and if reality fails to conform to theory, reality is rejected. The suffering is blamed on some unknown cause!

Another body that also assesses radiation risk is the BEIR Committee of the United States National Academy of Science. The BEIR (Biological Effects of Ionising Radiation) Committee was established in the United States around 1978 to counter accusations that the Nevada atmospheric nuclear tests had caused the deaths of thousands of American babies. BEIR is essentially a report and interpretation of the Hiroshima and Nagasaki studies of the effects of the atomic bomb, as previously discussed. These atomic bomb studies do not underpin the radiation standards, which actually were established some 17 years before the 1967 dose assessment for atomic bomb survivors, on which the atomic bomb studies are based, was completed.

The International Atomic Energy Agency radiation standards for nuclear waste were made 'on the basis of recommendations by a number of international bodies, principally the International Commission for Radiological Protection, and estimations of radiation risks made by the United Nations Scientific Committee on Atomic Radiation.' The International Atomic Energy Agency safety requirements for radioactive waste, including standards, codes of practice, regulations, and so on, 'may be adopted by Member States at their own discretion for use nationally'. These Agency requirements are mandatory *only* for the International Atomic Energy Agency itself.

What Happened to the People of Chernobyl?

One can easily imagine that there were civilian victims of radiation sickness in the midst of the chaos during and after the Chernobyl disaster who were never seen at Hospital Six in Moscow. However, the International Atomic Energy Agency continues, even in 2002, to insist that only 32 persons died of radiation exposure at Chernobyl! These 'counted' deaths were all men from the fire fighting brigade identified as seriously exposed and sick by the heroic physicians and other health personnel at the emergency medical tent near the crippled reactor. This type of counting goes even further than the usual mathematical and journalistic approach – it deliberately and maliciously minimises the scale of this disaster and leaves the public vulnerable. Those who were exposed suffer without appropriate medical recognition and help, while those at a distance remain unprepared for another, perhaps worse, disaster.

Moreover, since the land contaminated by the failed reactor was poisoned, the fruits and vegetables grown on it, and the domestic animals who feed on it, and their milk and meat, are also contaminated. Russia, Ukraine and Belarus have taken this contaminated food and, with the advice of the International Atomic Energy Agency, have mixed it with uncontaminated food from other parts of the former Soviet Union. This diluted (or adulterated) food has been given to the people to eat, subjecting them to continuous low doses of internal contamination with radionuclides for the last fifteen years. In Belarus, people actually received money from the government for moving back onto the badly contaminated areas and setting up new farms.

The false claims of the International Atomic Energy Agency have also failed to rally the international community to help the victims of this disaster. People have not responded internationally, with their characteristic generosity, to the tremendous needs of the people whose health and lives were cruelly disrupted. The International Atomic Energy Agency and its companion body, the United Nations Scientific Committee on the Effects of Atomic Radiation, have gone even further in the Spring of 2002, by recommending that Chechen and Central Asian refugees re-populate the still contaminated area around the failed reactor. This raises some very serious questions about the mismanagement of information and communication around this serious disaster.

These two United Nations agencies, namely the International Atomic Energy Agency and the United Nations Scientific Committee on Atomic Radiation, and their partner the International Commission on Radiological Protection, have apparently supplanted the World Health Organisation in speaking to the health risks of this nuclear technology, and in particular, to the post-Chernobyl contamination of the people and the land. Whether or not this land is fit for habitation, or for food production requires health assessment, not a promotional OK from two agencies which have financial ties to the polluting industry!

The World Health Organisation tried to take some initiative on behalf of the suffering people, and in 1996 its Director-General, Dr. Hiroshi Nakajima, organised in Geneva an international conference with 700 scientific experts and physicians, many of whom came from Russia, Belarus and Ukraine. The International Atomic Energy Agency, which to its dismay was not invited to jointly sponsor this international conference, nevertheless blocked publication of the proceedings. The physicians of Chernobyl then organised a conference in Kiev, Ukraine, in June 2001, and invited Dr. Nakajima (who was no longer Director-General of the World Health Organisation) to be their Honorary President. He was asked about the proceedings of the 1996 World Health Organisation Conference about the health of the Chernobyl victims which had never been published. He answered as follows: 'I was the Director-General and I was responsible. But it is mainly my legal department... Because the International Atomic Energy Agency reports directly to the Security Council of the United Nations...and we, all specialised organisations, report to the Economic and Social Development Council...the organisation which reports to the Security Council – not hierarchically, we are all equal – but for atomic affairs ... military use ... and peaceful or civil use ... they have the authority'.

Because of the internal United Nations structure, which is grossly out of date, the voice of the physicians and scientists actually dealing with the situation were not heard. It is outrageous to measure the radiation and then present a theory that no one has been hurt! It is imperative to look at the victims and assess their injury. Internationally, the theoretical voice of the International Commission on Radiological Protection, a non-governmental organisation, which speaks through the International Atomic Energy Agency and the United Nations Scientific Committee on Atomic Radiation, has prevailed. All three agencies have a vested interest in maintaining the reputation of nuclear industries as 'clean and cheap', even if they are not!

The representative of the United Nations Office for Humanitarian Affairs, D. Zupka, was present at the Kiev Conference, and he shared with participants the view of Kofi Annan, who estimated that the number of victims of Chernobyl is nine million. They are predicting that this number will increase. However, their voice is overpowered by the 'scientific' voice of the International Commission for Radiological Protection speaking through the International Atomic Energy Agency and the United Nations Scientific Committee on Atomic Radiation. This seems incredible, but is the heavy burden which we suffer as a legacy of the nuclear secrecy.

Because of the self-serving theoretical predictions and safety recommendations of the International Commission for Radiological Protection which colour the expectations of these radiologists, physicists and engineers, even when they are confronted with the reality of the suffering of the Chernobyl victims, these scientists strongly declare that the observed health problems could not be due to the radiation exposure. Health problems are instead assigned to an unidentified factor in the environment or life-style. Hans Blix, Director of the International Atomic Energy Agency at the time of the Chernobyl disaster, went so far as to say. 'The atomic industry can take catastrophes like Chernobyl every year'. There is an obvious conflict of interest for this agency mandated to promote nuclear technologies!

At the Kiev Conference, Alexey Yablokov, President of the Centre for Political Ecology of the Russian Federation, pointed out that the data used by the

United Nations Scientific Committee on Atomic Radiation had been falsified by the State Committee for Statistics, and the officials were arrested in 1999 for this crime. He charged that the United Nations Scientific Committee on Atomic Radiation continued to use this falsified data to support its minimisation of harm.

The medical research of Prof. Y Bandazhevsky, a medical pathologist, Rector of the Medical Institute of Gomel, in Belarus, had to be presented by a colleague, Prof. Michel Fernex. Prof. Bandazhevsky was under house arrest. Belarus received the heaviest fall out from the Chernobyl disaster. After nine years of research in Chernobyl-contaminated territories, he had discovered that caesium 137 incorporated in food, leads to destruction of those vital organs where the caesium 137 concentrates at higher than average body levels. With his wife, a paediatric cardiologist, Bandazhevsky described what he called 'caesium cardiomyopathy', and which others say is a syndrome which will eventually be named after him. The cardiac damage becomes irreversible at a certain level and duration of the caesium intoxication. Sudden death may occur at any age, even in children. After publishing this finding, denouncing government non-intervention policy, and arguing against the lack of resources given to the medical investigation of the disaster, Bandazhevsky was arrested, tried and condemned to prison for eight years.

The trial of Prof. Bandazhevsky was observed by lawyers from the Organisation for Security and Co-operation in Europe (OSCE), from the French Embassy in Minsk, and from Amnesty International. These observers documented irregularities and legal errors from the time of his arrest. In the middle of the night of July 13, 1999, Prof. Bandazhevsky was arrested by a group of police officers, who informed him that the arrest was by presidential decree aimed at fighting terrorism. This was never charged in court. In fact, it was not until four weeks after his arrest, August 1999, that he was finally charged with taking bribes. These proved to be trumped up charges by two defendants who later recanted their testimony saying it was forced under duress and threats. Prof. Bandazhevsky was denied access to a lawyer for the entire duration of his detention, and during the trial there were serious breaches of Belarussian and international law. Amnesty International has listed Prof. Bandazhevsky as a prisoner of conscience. He is not well, and his important research is being kept from his scientific and medical colleagues.

Professor Bandazhevsky is not alone. The Russian, Belarussian, and Ukrainian medical community, though silenced in international circles, was still present and active in alleviating the suffering and noting the causes of their people's pain. Many have carried out detailed high quality scientific studies on the genetic, teratogenic and somatic damage done by radiation exposure. They have confirmed their analyses by demonstrating the effects in animal experiments. The rest of the world is being deprived of this research through heavy handed silencing of the scientists by their national authorities, acting on the recommendations of the International Atomic Energy Agency and the United

Nations Scientific Committee on Atomic Radiation, and especially the International Commission on Radiological Protection.

Recommendations

While many individuals have been trying to make known this major United Nations problem, it has been difficult to get this complex situation across to the public in 'sound bites'. Serious study on the part of the United Nations will be needed to undo all of the damage caused. However, it seems possible to make the following recommendations to the United Nations:

- The World Health Organisation should be mandated to review all radiation research and to recommend health-based safety regulations. This mandate should be carried out by health professionals, including epidemiologists, oncologists, occupational and public health specialists, geneticists and paediatricians, (not linked with the nuclear industries or nuclear medicine), rather than other scientists.
- The International Atomic Energy Agency mandate to promote 'peaceful nuclear technologies' should be withdrawn.
- The International Atomic Energy Agency mandate to safeguard the spread of nuclear weapons should be expanded to include monitoring the reduction and abolition of all nuclear weapons in the nuclear nations.
- The United Nations Scientific Committee on Atomic Radiation (UNSCEAR) mandate needs to include the monitoring of increasing levels of background radiation and nuclear emissions from reactors and nuclear accidents. They should not be entrusted with estimating risk, which is the prerogative of the World Health Organisation.
- Decisions relative to the safety of farmland, food and water ingestion and refugee relocation should be entrusted to the World Health Organisation.
- Investigation into the imprisonment of scientists and physicians who have spoken out on behalf of the public health relative to radiation exposure should be undertaken by a special rapporteur of the Human Rights Commission in Geneva.

With grateful acknowledgements to the Journal of Humanitarian Medicine.

Amicus fighting for the liberty of working people at home and abroad

Joint General Secretary
Derek Simpson

Joint General Secretary
Roger Lyons

THE BERTRAND RUSSELL PEACE FOUNDATION
PEACE DOSSIER

CENSORED IRAQI DECLARATION

As we reported in the last Peace Dossier, the overwhelmingly larger part of Iraq's report on weapons of mass destruction was withheld from the elected members of the United Nations Security Council. The Russell Foundation is still seeking an explanation of how this censorship came about, who did it, and on what mandate. The following letters and newspaper report take the story further.

The Times, February 13, 2003
Weapons declaration
From Professor Ken Coates
Sir, Jack Straw claims that Iraq's declaration about its weapons of mass destruction, submitted to the United Nations in December, 'was neither full, accurate, nor complete' (Comment, February 5).

The elected members of the United Nations Security Council will have to take Mr Straw's word for it, since we understand that more than 8,000 of the declaration's 11,800 pages were omitted when it was circulated to them.

The full dossier was given to the United Nations and transported to New York, where by some mechanism it came into the hands of the United States Administration, which promised to copy it for members of the Security Council. In the event, two thirds of the declaration were withheld from the ten non-permanent members. I wrote to these members asking whether British press reports on these matters were true (an inquiry to the office of the Secretary-General had produced no response).

The current President of the Security Council, Joschka Fischer, confirmed these facts. In a letter dated Monday, February 3, his office writes:

> 'The facts of the case as you present them are correct. In fact the Iraqi statement of around 12,000 pages of 8th December was given in full only to the five permanent members of the Security Council.'

Who authorised this substantial deletion?

Yours sincerely,
Ken Coates
Chairman, Bertrand Russell Peace Foundation

The Times, February 18, 2003
From Mr Llew Smith, MP for Blaenau Gwent (Labour)

Sir, Professor Ken Coates asks (letter, February 13th) who authorised the deletion of 8,000 pages of Iraq's original declaration to the United Nations last December, prior to its distribution to non-permanent UN Security Council members.

I asked the Foreign Secretary about this removal of information in a written question, to which I received the following reply from junior Foreign Office Minister, Denis MacShane:

> The President of the UN Security Council decided that the Iraqi Declaration should first be given to [permanent] members of the Security Council with the expertise to assess the risks of proliferation… UNMOVIC and the IAEA will judge what material needs to be excised before it distributes the declaration to all Security Council members (Hansard, December 17, 2002, col.764W).

While I can accept the sensitivity of some of the details in the Iraqi declaration, which could contain information on how to make certain weapons of mass destruction, I do not accept that the diplomatic delegations of member states of the United Nations Security Council would be unable to keep confidential information that should remain so.

I prefer the suggestion made at the time (report, December 12) that the Iraqi declaration named US and UK suppliers to Iraq's military programme that our Governments did not want made public, as it would show direct complicity in building up Saddam's weapons arsenal.

Yours sincerely,
Llew Smith
House of Commons, February 13.

The Times, February 26, 2003
Implications of weapons dossier cuts
From Professor Ken Coates

Sir, In his response to my letter published on February 13, Llew Smith, MP (letter, February 18), throws a further interesting light on the suppression of two thirds of the Iraqi dossier on weapons of mass destruction which was submitted to the United Nations on December 7.

However, I have recently received more informative letters from the Swedish Foreign Secretary and from Hans von Sponeck, the former Assistant Secretary-General to the UN who resigned in protest at UN policy in 2000, who is glad that this matter has now emerged into the public domain.

On December 7 the presidency of the Security Council was held by Colombia. I understand that the United States deployed all the arts of persuasion to ensure that Colombia yielded up the Iraqi dossier on the implausible pretext that the

Americans had superior photocopying facilities to those which were available in the United Nations Secretariat. I still have not been able to elicit precise information about how the suppression of so much of the dossier was decided. But there is a more serious matter.

Both the British and Swedish Foreign Offices agree that the permanent members of the Security Council were involved in transferring to Unmovic and the IAEA the decision about what to excise. But the Swedish Foreign Minister registers the opinion that the Security Council cannot risk having an A team and a B team, one of which is informed, and the other not.

Certainly the permanent members have a special status in respect of voting, but they have no constitutionally valid special status in terms of access to information, or rights to withhold inconvenient information from their colleagues.

This raises a vital principle. As Hans von Sponeck writes in his letter to me:

> It is not only a case of unacceptable differential treatment of permanent and non-permanent members of the UN Security Council, it is also a challenge to the neutrality of the UN Secretariat.

Yours sincerely,
Ken Coates

* * *

Revealed: 17 British firms armed Saddam with his weapons

Neil Mackay, Sunday Herald, 2/24/03
http://www.sundayherald.com/31710

Seventeen British companies who supplied Iraq with nuclear, biological, chemical, rocket and conventional weapons technology are to be investigated and could face prosecution following a Sunday Herald investigation.

One of the companies is International Military Services, a part of the Ministry of Defence, which sold rocket technology to Iraq. The companies were named by Iraq in a 12,000 page dossier submitted to the UN in December. The Security Council agreed to US requests to censor 8000 pages – including sections naming western businesses which aided Iraq's weapons of mass destruction programme.

The five permanent members of the security council – Britain, France, Russia, America and China – are named as allowing companies to sell weapons technology to Iraq.

The dossier claims 24 US firms sold Iraq weapons. Hewlett-Packard sold nuclear and rocket technology; Dupont sold nuclear technology; and Eastman Kodak sold rocket capabilities. The dossier also says some '50 subsidiaries of foreign enterprises conducted their arms business with Iraq from the US'...

TORTURE ON DIEGO GARCIA?

In our previous issue, we examined press reports about the interrogation and torture of a number of captives said to be members of Al Qaeda, or holding other allegiances. In particular, an article in the *Washington Post (26.12.02)* quite specifically alleged that the United States has 'rendered' captives for interrogation in a number of other countries in which the conventions about torture are said to be more laxly interpreted. Such countries include Egypt, Jordan, Syria and Yemen.

But the *Washington Post* also quite specifically alleged that unjustifiable interrogation techniques were being used at the US bases of Bagram in Afghanistan, and on the small island of Diego Garcia in the Indian Ocean. Diego Garcia has the status of a British Indian Ocean Territory. It is leased by the United States who use it as a strategic military base. There is no British Civilian Administration on Diego Garcia. The island usually has a small complement of less than 50 Royal Naval personnel under a Royal Navy Commander who also acts as the representative of the British Foreign Office.

When the allegations of torture on Diego Garcia were raised in the British House of Lords, on 8 January 2003, Baroness Amos, the Foreign Office Minister, denied them. She said 'The United States Government would need to ask for our permission to bring any suspects to Diego Garcia. It has not done so, and no suspected terrorists are being held on Diego Garcia... under current British Indian Ocean Territory law, there would be no authority for the detention of Al Qaeda suspects in the territory.'

A further enquiry elicited a response from Charles Hamilton of the Overseas Territories Department in the Foreign & Commonwealth Office who replied that: 'Under the various treaties governing the use of Diego Garcia by the US, they would have to ask for our permission before they could hold suspected terrorists there. As Baroness Amos said in the House of Lords on 8 January, they have not done so, and they have assured us that there is no truth in the press stories.'

In our last issue, we promised to look into this denial of torture on Diego Garcia. We sought a response from the *Washington Post* to Baroness Amos's original statement. Barton Gellman, one of the journalists responsible for the article of 26 December, informed us that he saw no reason to modify their story. He wrote:

> 'Our experience with spokesmen most likely mirrors yours: they persuade themselves sometimes that they avoid a lie (while appearing to call something true false) by using private definitions of ordinary language. The formulation of Baroness Amos might be consistent with a view that those being held are not suspected "terrorists" but perhaps "associates" of some organisation, or that being held aboard a ship is not "on" Diego Garcia. (I don't know if they're aboard ship or not.) Or again that those present are not "held" because they've voluntarily agreed to be questioned there in lieu of transfer to some place nastier.
>
> A more complex statement – referring to a secret base for interrogation and torture

– might be denied with many things in mind. The spokesman might maintain an unspoken view that the methods of questioning don't count as torture, and therefore that the entire sentence is wrong because it uses "and" to link interrogation to torture. I don't know what was in the minds of your officials, but I do not exaggerate the way the game is now played in Washington.

What we have from our sources is that some al Qaeda suspects are indeed being held and questioned at Diego Garcia. The British government could go some way to clearing this up by permitting you or us to pay an unrestricted visit. If I had anything else I could tell you I would publish it, and I haven't.'

SPYING ON THE UNITED NATIONS – READ ALL ABOUT IT?

Norman Solomon examines the suppression of a crucial story by the media in the United States.

Three days after a British newspaper revealed a memo about the United States spying on United Nations Security Council delegations, I asked Daniel Ellsberg to assess the importance of the story. 'This leak,' he replied, 'is more timely and potentially more important than the Pentagon Papers.'

The key word is 'timely.' Publication of the secret Pentagon Papers in 1971, made possible by Ellsberg's heroic decision to leak those documents, came after the Vietnam War had already been under way for many years. But with all-out war on Iraq still in the future, the leak about spying at the United Nations could erode the Bush administration's already slim chances of getting a war resolution through the Security Council.

'As part of its battle to win votes in favour of war against Iraq,' the London-based *Observer* reported on March 2 that the United States government developed an 'aggressive surveillance operation, which involves interception of the home and office telephones and the e-mails of United Nations delegates.' The smoking gun was 'a memorandum written by a top official at the National Security Agency – the U.S. body which intercepts communications around the world – and circulated to both senior agents in his organisation and to a friendly foreign intelligence agency.'

The Observer added: 'The leaked memorandum makes clear that the target of the heightened surveillance efforts are the delegations from Angola, Cameroon, Chile, Mexico, Guinea and Pakistan at the UN headquarters in New York – the so-called 'Middle Six' delegations whose votes are being fought over by the pro-war party, led by the US and Britain, and the party arguing for more time for UN inspections, led by France, China and Russia.'

The National Security Agency memo, dated January 31, outlines the wide scope of the surveillance activities, seeking any information useful to push a war resolution through the Security Council – 'the whole gamut of information that could give US policymakers an edge in obtaining results favourable to US goals or to head off surprises.'

Three days after the memo came to light, *The Times* of London printed an article noting that the Bush administration 'finds itself isolated' in its zeal for war on Iraq. 'In the most recent setback,' the newspaper reported, 'a memorandum by the US National Security Agency, leaked to *The Observer*, revealed that American spies were ordered to eavesdrop on the conversations of the six undecided countries on the United Nations Security Council.'

The London *Times* article called it an 'embarrassing disclosure.' And the embarrassment was nearly world-wide. From Russia to France to Chile to Japan to Australia, the story was big mainstream news. But not in the United States.

Several days after the 'embarrassing disclosure,' not a word about it had appeared in America's supposed paper of record. *The New York Times* – the single most influential media outlet in the United States – still had not printed anything about the story. How could that be?

'Well, it's not that we haven't been interested,' *New York Times* deputy foreign editor Alison Smale said on the evening of March 5, nearly 96 hours after *The Observer* broke the story. 'We could get no confirmation or comment' on the memo from US officials.

The New York Times opted not to relay *The Observer's* account, Smale told me. 'We would normally expect to do our own intelligence reporting.' She added: 'We are still definitely looking into it. It's not that we're not.'

Belated coverage would be better than none at all. But readers should be suspicious of the failure of *The New York Times* to cover this story during the crucial first days after it broke. At some moments in history, when war and peace hang in the balance, journalism delayed is journalism denied.

Overall, the sparse US coverage that did take place seemed eager to downplay the significance of *The Observer's* revelations. On March 4, the *Washington Post* ran a back-page 514-word article headlined 'Spying Report No Shock to UN,' while the *Los Angeles Times* published a longer piece that began by emphasising that US spy activities at the United Nations are 'long-standing.'

The US media treatment has contrasted sharply with coverage on other continents. 'While some have taken a ho-hum attitude in the US, many around the world are furious,' says Ed Vulliamy, one of *The Observer* reporters who wrote the March 2 article. 'Still, almost all governments are extremely reluctant to speak up against the espionage. This further illustrates their vulnerability to the US government.'

To Daniel Ellsberg, the leaking of the National Security Agency memo was a hopeful sign. 'Truth-telling like this can stop a war,' he said. Time is short for insiders at intelligence agencies 'to tell the truth and save many many lives.' But major news outlets must stop dodging the information that emerges.

Norman Solomon is co-author of the new book '*Target Iraq: What the News Media Didn't Tell You*,' published by Context Books (www.contextbooks.com/newF.html).

'SHOCK AND AWE' WAR ON IRAQ

Vladimir Slipchenko, military analyst, doctor of military sciences, professor, and a major general in the reserves, is a leading Russian specialist on future wars. His predictions of the course of United States military operations in Iraq (1991, 1996, and 1998), Yugoslavia (1999), and Afghanistan (2001) coincided closely with what subsequently happened. Here, he predicts the course and outcome of the next United States war against Iraq, which the American military themselves have already dubbed Operation 'Shock and Awe.' Vladimir Slipchenko is interviewd by Aleksandr Khokhlov of Rossiyskaya Gazeta.

Vladimir Ivanovich, so much has already been said about the reasons and causes of the new war in Iraq, but I cannot get rid of the feeling that they are either talking about something entirely different, or not telling the full story?

The main purpose of the war is indeed being left out of the picture and nobody is saying anything about it. I see the main purpose of the war as being the large-scale real-life testing by the United States of sophisticated models of precision weapons. That is the objective that they place first. All the other aims are either incidental, or outright disinformation.

For more than ten years now, the United States has conducted exclusively no-contact wars. In May 2001, George Bush Junior, delivering his first presidential speech to students at the Naval Academy in Annapolis, spoke of the need for accelerated preparation of the United States Armed Forces for future wars. He emphasised that they should be high-tech Armed Forces capable of conducting hostilities throughout the world by the no-contact method. This task is now being carried out very consistently.

It should be observed that the Pentagon buys from the military-industrial complex only those weapons that have been tested in conditions of real warfare and received a certificate of quality on the battlefield. After a series of live experiments – the wars in Iraq, Yugoslavia, and Afghanistan – many corporations in the United States military-industrial complex have been granted the right to sell their precision weapons to the Pentagon. They include Lockheed Martin, General Electric, and Loral. But many other well-known companies are as yet without orders from the military department. The bottom line is $50-60 billion a year. Who would want to miss out on that kind of money? But the present suppliers of precision weapons to the Pentagon are also constantly developing new types of arms and they must also be tested The United States military-industrial complex demands test-bed wars from its country's political leadership. And it gets them. And that is the main aim of the new war in Iraq.

How will this war differ from the no-contact wars previously waged by the United States?

First, in terms of its political objectives. For the first time since 1991, the United States sets the goal of changing the political system in the enemy state and removing or physically eliminating the country's leadership. They have not previously succeeded in this. Remember, the Americans did not previously try to remove Saddam Hussein from politics, and even Milosevic was not removed from the post of Yugoslav leader by military means. The United States Armed Forces carried out their required tests of new weapons and then packed up their guns and went home. Now they face a very difficult mission. Therefore, second, because of the change of objective the strategy of the war also changes radically. For the first time the war aims mean that the United States must without fail achieve total victory. To that end it is necessary to achieve three objectives: rout the enemy's armed forces, destroy his economy, and change the political system.

The Iraqi army will be subjected to very powerful blows. It will be physically annihilated. In order to impose a new puppet government in the country (and I am sure the Americans have already formed that government) and to give that government the opportunity to get on with its work, the United States will be forced actually to occupy Iraq. The occupation of territory within which seats of organised resistance could persist would lead to large losses among US Army personnel. Guerrillas, and in the context of the Arab world also *shahid* martyrs wearing explosive belts – naturally the Americans do not need this Therefore they will totally annihilate the Iraqi army. Practically all Iraq servicemen will die. There will be terrible carnage.

Does Iraq have any chance of offering resistance to the United States?

In Iraq we will once again see a situation where two generations of warfare meet. Iraq is strong and prepared for a war of the last generation – on land and for land, for every target. But 600,000 soldiers, 220 military aircraft, something like 2,200 tanks, 1,900 artillery guns, around 500 multiple rocket launchers, 6 SCUD missile launchers, 110 surface-to-air missile systems, and 700 anti-aircraft installations will prove useless when they meet the aggressor. In fact, there will not be a meeting on the battlefield as such. The Americans, waging a no-contact war, will methodically use precision missile strikes to destroy all the key facilities of Iraq's state and military infrastructure, and will then wipe out enemy manpower with missile and bombing raids.

How will the Americans begin hostilities?

First of all there will be precision strikes against bunkers and command posts where Saddam Hussein and the Iraqi leaders might be hiding, against Army headquarters and troop positions, and against components of the air defence system. Sophisticated ground-penetrating vacuum-type precision munitions will be used to destroy buried targets. Even if one of these weapons explodes not exactly inside, say, an underground bunker, in any case the exits from the shelter will be blocked. The bunker will become a mass grave for everyone who is unfortunate enough to be in it.

To destroy armoured equipment, in the very first days the Americans will use cluster aviation bombs with self-guided munitions. The 'mother'-cluster bomb gives 'birth' to several tens or hundreds of 'baby' bombs, each of which independently chooses its own target to destroy on the ground. I am confident that in the very first hours of the war the United States will also use new pulse bombs They are also called microwave bombs. The principle on which these weapons operate is as follows: there is an instantaneous discharge of electromagnetic radiation of the order of two megawatts. At a distance of 2-2.5 kilometres from the epicentre of the explosion the 'microwaves' instantly put out of action all radio-electronic systems, communications and radar systems, all computers, radio receivers, and even hearing aids and heart pacemakers. All these things are destroyed by the meltdown method. Just imagine, a person's heart explodes!

As a result of the use of these weapons, Iraqi systems for command and control of the state and troops will be destroyed practically instantaneously.

What other new types of arms could be tested?

Since this war will be experimental for the United States, several new types of precision cruise missiles will be tested with a view to obtaining quality certificates. I believe attention will be devoted first and foremost to missile launches from submarines. The Americans are planning to make their submarine fleet the main launch-pad. The Pentagon will continue to perfect the mechanism for targeting precision weapons. In 2000, with the help of the space shuttle *Endeavour*, the United States scanned around 80 per cent of the surface of the Earth and created an electronic map of the planet in three-dimensional co-ordinates. The level of detail of objects on this map is down to the size of a window. That is to say, you could train a lens – installed in a military satellite – first on Baghdad, then on the city centre, then on Saddam's palace, and on his bedroom window. You give the command – and in a few minutes' time a targeted cruise missile flies into that window.

How long will this war go on?

I predict that Operation Shock And Awe will last not more than six weeks. The first period of the war – the 'shock' – will last around 30 days. Some 400-500 sea and air-based precision cruise missiles will be launched against targets in Iraq every 24 hours. During that month Iraq's troops and its economic potential will be annihilated. Anything that survives for any reason will be guaranteed destruction in the next two weeks. In the second stage – 'awe' – the Americans will conduct a piloted version of a total clean-up of the territory. To this end the United States will use B-52 and B-2 Stealth bombers. In four hours of flight one Stealth is capable of detecting and destroying as many as 200 stationary or moving targets on the ground. The United States intends to use at least 16 B-2 bombers. The Stealths will be in the air constantly, one replacing the other.

Will the Iraqi air defence system be able to counter the American planes and cruise missiles?

Iraq already has no air defence facilities in the north and south of the country – United States aviation is constantly bombing these areas. What remains in the centre of the country will be destroyed in the first 10 minutes of the war. Iraq's anti-aircraft system is based on the classical active radar detection system: emit – detect – illuminate – destroy. The Americans will exploit this for their own purposes. As soon as an Iraqi radar reveals itself by emitting electromagnetic energy, a precision cruise missile will be dispatched against the 'revealed' air defence facility using this same beam. Iraq has no chance of countering this.

How much will this war cost?

According to my estimates, $80 billion. But the total sum spent could rise to 100 billion. We will never know the exact figure of expenditure, if only because the war will be partly funded by private companies offering the Pentagon their experimental models of precision weapons for free in the hope of future dividends. The programme for rearming the US Armed Forces is about $600 billion Therefore, the military-industrial complex need not stint. It can give weapons to the Army for free.

What human losses could Iraq suffer?

Very considerable ones. Since the Americans are planning to physically annihilate the Iraqi army, I reckon that at least 500,000 people will be killed. This will be a very bloody war.

What will come after the war?

The Americans will have to occupy Iraq. The occupation corps will apparently consist of four mechanised and armoured divisions, one parachute division, and one division of the British Armed Forces. All these troops will not fight. There will be no ground operations in Iraq! The US Army will enter a burning desert – the Iraqis will certainly set fire to the oilfields – without a single shot being fired. There will simply be nobody to shoot at them.

How long will the direct occupation last? Will the Americans stay in Iraq forever?

They will certainly leave Iraq. There is no point in their staying there. The occupation will last one and a half, two, or at the most three years and will cost American taxpayers a further $80-100 billion to maintain the troops in Iraq. Then the United States may enlist in an operation that they will undoubtedly call 'peacekeeping' the Poles, Czechs, and other 'new recruits' to NATO, the Estonians, but they themselves will leave. The 'peacekeepers' will stay a further one to one and a half years in Iraq.

During this time major investments will be made in the country with a regime friendly to the United States, and in two years' time Iraq's oil sector will reach a level of oil extraction of 2-2.4 million barrels a day. In five years they will be extracting up to 5 million barrels of oil a day. The world oil price will fall to $12-15 a barrel. The currently stagnant United States economy will soar.

And what will happen to Russia's economy, which is currently supported exclusively by 'petrodollars'?

I have no answer to that question. I am an expert in wars.

© Rossiyskaya Gazeta 2003

AGAINST PRE-EMPTION

The International Association of Lawyers against Nuclear Arms issued their international appeal in February 2003 (see www.ialana.org).

We the undersigned lawyers and jurists from legal traditions around the world are extremely concerned about conflicts in the Middle East regarding the suspected proliferation of weapons of mass destruction, and the possibility that force may be used in response to this situation.

The development of weapons of mass destruction anywhere in the world is contrary to universal norms against the acquisition, possession and threat or use of such weapons and must be addressed. However, the 'preventive' use of force currently being considered against Iraq is both illegal and unnecessary and should not be authorised by the United Nations or undertaken by any State.

General principles of international law hold that:
- peaceful resolution of conflicts between States is required,
- the use of force is only permissible in the case of an armed attack or imminent attack or under UN authorisation when a threat to the peace has been declared by the Security Council and non-military measures have been determined to be inadequate,
- enforcement of international law must be consistently applied to all States

In further enunciating and applying these principles, we believe that the use of force against Iraq would be illegal for the following reasons:

Peaceful resolution of conflicts required

i. The United Nations Charter and customary international law require States to seek peaceful resolutions to their disputes. Article 33 of the Charter states that 'The parties to any dispute, the continuance of which is likely to endanger the maintenance of international peace and security, shall first of all seek a solution by negotiation, enquiry, mediation, conciliation, arbitration, judicial settlement, resort to regional agencies or arrangements or other peaceful means of their own choice.'

ii. Under Article 51 of the Charter, States are only permitted to threaten or use force 'if an armed attack occurs' and only 'until the Security Council has taken measures necessary to maintain international peace and security.'

iii. In the case of an act of aggression or a threat to the peace, the United Nations Security Council is also required under the Charter (Article 41) to firstly employ 'measures not involving the use of armed force.' Only when such measures 'would be inadequate or have proved to be inadequate' (Article 42) can the Security Council authorise the use of force.

No act of aggression or evidence of imminent threat of such act

iv. In 1991 the Security Council responded to an actual invasion of Kuwait by Iraq by authorising all means necessary to restore the peace. In the current case, however, there has been no indication by Iraq that it intends to attack another country and no evidence of military preparations for any such attack. In addition, it is generally recognized that Iraq does not have the military capability to attack the key countries in dispute, i.e. the United States and the United Kingdom.

No precedent for preventive use of force

v. There is no precedent in international law for use of force as a preventive measure when there has been no actual or imminent attack by the offending State. There is law indicating that preventive use of force is illegal. The International Military Tribunal sitting at Nuremberg rejected Germany's argument that they were compelled to attack Norway in order to prevent an Allied invasion (6 F.R.D. 69, 100-101, 1946).

vi. The Security Council has never authorised force based on a potential, non-imminent threat of violence. All past authorisations have been in response to actual invasion, large scale violence or humanitarian emergency.

vii. If the Security Council, for the first time, were to authorise preventive war, it would undermine the UN Charter's restraints on the use of force and provide a dangerous precedent for States to consider the 'preventive' use of force in numerous situations, making war once again a tool of international politics rather than an anachronistic and prohibited action. If the use of force takes place outside the framework of international law and the UN Charter, the structure and authority of international law and the UN Charter, which have taken generations and immense human sacrifice to establish, would be severely undermined into the foreseeable future.

Consistency under international law must be maintained

viii. International law must be consistently applied in order to maintain the respect of the international community as law and not the rejection of it as a tool of the powerful to subjugate the weak.

ix. Security Council Resolution 687, setting forth the terms of the ceasefire that ended the Gulf War, acknowledges that the elimination of Iraq's weapons of mass destruction is not an end in itself but 'represents steps towards the goal of establishing in the Middle East a zone free from weapons of mass destruction.'

x. The International Court of Justice has unanimously determined that there is an obligation on all States to 'pursue in good faith and bring to a conclusion negotiations leading to nuclear disarmament in all its aspects under strict and effective international control.' (*Legality of the Threat or Use of Nuclear Weapons, ICJ 1996*). Meaningful steps need to be taken by all States to this end, and States wishing to enforce compliance with international law must themselves comply with this requirement.

xi. Action to ensure the elimination of Iraq's weapons of mass destruction should be done in conjunction with similar actions to ensure elimination of other weapons of mass destruction in the region – including Israel's nuclear arsenal – and in the world – including the nuclear weapons of China, France, India, Pakistan, Russia, United Kingdom and the United States.

Alternative mechanisms are available to address concerns

xii. The UN Security Council has established a number of mechanisms to address the concerns regarding Iraqi weapons of mass destruction. These include diplomatic pressure, negotiations, sanctions on certain goods with military application, destruction of stockpiles of weapons of mass destruction and inspections of facilities with capabilities to assist in production of weapons of mass destruction. Evidence to date is that these mechanisms are not perfect, but are working effectively enough to have led to the destruction and curtailment of most of the Iraqi weapons of mass destruction capability.

xiii. Mechanisms are available to address charges against Iraq and the Iraqi leadership of serious human rights violations, war crimes, crimes against peace and crimes against humanity. These include domestic courts utilising universal jurisdiction, the establishment by the Security Council of an ad hoc international criminal tribunal, use of the International Criminal Court for any crimes committed after July 2002, and the International Court of Justice.

The use of force by powerful nations in disregard of the principles of international law would threaten the fabric of international law giving rise to the potential for further violations and an increasing cycle of violence and anarchy.

We call on the United Nations and all States to continue to pursue a path of adherence to international law and in pursuit of a peaceful resolution to the threats arising from weapons of mass destruction and other threats to the peace.

DUNCAN SMITH

We have been saddened to notice the death of Duncan Smith, not IDS, but the author of one of the latest 'Socialist Renewal' pamphlets, which he entitled

Physician, Heal Thyself (2002). The pamphlet was an updating of proposals which he had made when he was Chief Training Officer for the NHS to establish a National Health Service Staff College. Now that the NHS has a University and a Vice-Chancellor, it is to be hoped that Duncan Smith's enthusiasm for workers' control (he called it 'participation'), which he had gained over many years as the Training Officer for the National Coal Board, will take a central place in the studies at this new university. His best known work was *In Search of Social Justice* (1995) which introduced readers to the intellectual and ethical roots of the New Economic Foundation's 'philosophy based on justice, sustainability, community and democracy'.

GIVE PEACE A CHANCE

The New Rulers of the World
JOHN PILGER

'Pilger is unique not just for his undimmed anger but also for the sharpness of his focus, the range of targets that he chooses and the meticulous precision with which he hits them – often with their own words.' **New Internationalist**

$13/£8 pbk / 1-85984-412-X / 246 pages / Forthcoming April 2003
$19/£10 hbk / 1-85984-393-X / 192 pages / Available now

War Plan Iraq
Ten Reasons Against War on Iraq
MILAN RAI

'Give peace a chance and buy this book. Milan Rai's superb dossier explains why Bush's proposed war against Iraq has little to do with Saddam's tyranny and everything to do with Washington's infinite greed for oil and power.' **Mike Davis**

$15/£10 pbk / 1-85984-501-0 / 256 pages / Available now

The Clash of Fundamentalisms
Crusades, Jihads and Modernity
TARIQ ALI

'In this timely and important book, Tariq Ali puts the events of September 11 into sweeping historical perspective. As we have come to expect from him, he is lucid, eloquent, literary, and painfully honest, as he dissects both Islamic and Western fundamentalism.' **Howard Zinn**

$15/£10 pbk / 1-85984-457-X / 375 pages / Forthcoming April
$22/£15 hbk / 1-85984-679-3 / 342 pages / Available now

VERSO

VERSO BOOKS ARE AVAILABLE FROM ALL GOOD BOOKSHOPS, OR LOG ON TO www.versobooks.com

Reviews

Devil's Rope

Olivier Razac, (translated by Jonathan Kneight), *Barbed Wire: A History*, Profile Books, 148 pages, ISBN 186 197 455 8, £6.99

In this concise and copiously illustrated, postcard-sized book French philosopher Olivier Razac has produced an absorbing and thoroughly invigorating history of the 'devil's rope.' Razac might not be the first to interpret enclosure as an unambiguously political act which 'marks out the boundaries of private property, assists in the effective management of land, and makes social distinctions concrete.' Indeed, his thesis, that barbed wire polarises and delimits space, effectively demarcating 'a threatening exterior and a protective interior' may appear familiar to many. However, it is in his application of this analysis to barbed wire's crucial historical role in creating spaces of life affirming inclusion and murderous exclusion which really distinguishes Razac's book.

Although *Barbed Wire* makes no pretence to provide a comprehensive history, Razac's choice of three historical 'landmarks' where 'the clearest and most significant political implications' of its use can be seen, are particularly apposite: the American prairie, the trenches of the First World War and the Nazi concentration camps. Charting it's evolution from seemingly benign agricultural tool to 'the frontier between life and death,' Razac notes that the key ingredient in the prolonged success of barbed wire has been due not to technical refinement but rather its unerring simplicity. Barbed wire as we know it today was the invention of Joseph F. Glidden, an Illinois farmer whose 1874 innovation engendered a 'veritable revolution' on the prairie by providing incoming settlers with a cheap, durable way of colonising inhospitable land and protecting it from herds of cattle, thus accelerating Westward expansion through the Great Plains; a process which, thanks largely to barbed wire, was completed within twenty years.

But the popularity of barbed wire was not without consequence. America was not, as the philosopher John Locke suggested, *terra nulius*. However, such sentiments had a devastating effect for they eventually enclosed the Indian, his lands and his civilisation out of existence. And deliberately so for the enclosure of the Great Plains heralded the arrival of private property and the demise of the communal patterns of land ownership which characterised Indian civilisation. Together with the railroad and a handful of government edicts legalising the theft of tribal lands, barbed wire played an integral role in the ruthless pulverisation of Indian civilisation, forcing it further and further to the geographical margins until it could exist no more. Ironically, it also led to the collapse of the 'cattle empire' amidst a series of 'barbed-wire wars.' When the open range disappeared, so too did that quintessentially American figure, the cowboy. The attendant irony, that the (mythic) cowboy has come to be imbued with precisely those attributes which barbed wire and genocide succeeded in eradicating, is not lost upon Razac.

Moving to the First World War, Razac, a Frenchman, concentrates perhaps unsurprisingly upon the experience of *Les Poilus* and particularly the iconography of *les barbelés* as revealed in the newsletters of their veterans associations. The psychological and physical suffering caused by barbed wire is indelibly etched onto memories of its survivors, and in this sense has become part of the 'aesthetic' of the battlefield. Indeed Razac might easily have chosen any nation as his subject, for the encounter of the deadly impenetrability of the 'cruel tangles' (Siegfried Sassoon) was universal. Virtually invulnerable to artillery fire, barbed wire was lethal for those troops unfortunate enough to be caught upon this 'unplashed hedge' where untold legions 'paid the bill' (Edmund Blunden).

As Razac also shows, barbed wire supplied the 'central element' in the architecture of the Nazis concentration camps where 'it provided the essential foundation of the totalitarian management of space.' Here the use of barbed wire aided immeasurably the 'physical realisation' of Nazi genocide. As a graphic symbol of political violence and barbarous captivity (electrified) barbed wire served to stigmatise, atomise and compartmentalise the inmates of the concentration camp by dividing nationalities and races both from 'normal society' and one another, exacerbating their dehumanisation in the process and causing barbed wire to revert to its original purpose: the enclosure 'animals' worthy only of annihilation.

Since 1945 barbed wire has continued to oppress. Indeed the skeletal figures behind the barbed wire fences of Omarsk in Yugoslavia provided a pungent reminder of the long shadow of racial barbarity stalking Europe's recent past. Yet the anxiety caused by such images has failed to stop barbed wire enveloping the occupied territories, or the multiplicity of refugee camps which radiate from it. Barbed wire it seems is destined to remain omnipresent even within Europe whose own frontiers, though no longer ringed by barbed wire, contain pockets of a hostile 'exterior' which proliferate in the form of 'reception centres' and 'holding camps' for refugees and asylum seekers. Perhaps it is nowhere more prevalent than in Cyprus where 115 miles of barbed wire mark the 'last wall in Europe.'

Yet, despite this continued ubiquity, Razac makes a number of astute observations regarding the future modalities of repression. Barbed wire, argues Razac, came into being at a 'decisive stage' in history when 'power was already rejecting the thickness of stones, massive separations, to create territorial divisions.' Thus light, mobile and temporal razor wire replaced ramparts. However, whilst barbed wire has remained a potent symbol of oppression, (indeed one need look no further than Amnesty International's logo), barbed wire has become intensely unpopular; to compensate, more 'ethereal means' of controlling space have been found. Optical and electronic surveillance, of which face recognition technology is only the most obvious manifestation, have begun to segregate our shopping precincts and communities, argues Razac, intensifying our immobility and creating a socio-economic and racial 'no man's-land' into which human refuse is consigned. Although these exclusive social hierarchies are well hidden by such 'discreet violence', they are no less rigidly organised for their invisibility. As Razac cogently argues, our walls may now be made of glass rather than barbed wire, but they are walls nonetheless.

Graham Macklin

Christian Empires

Niall Ferguson, *Empire: How Britain Made The Modern World***, Allen Lane, 392 pages, hardback ISBN 0713996153 £25**
Arthur Herman, *The Scottish Enlightenment: The Scots' Invention of the Modern World***, Fourth Estate, 454 pages, paperback ISBN 1841152765 £8.99**

'The Europeans came to our land with their Bibles; and they taught us to close our eyes and pray, and when we opened our eyes, we had the Bibles and they had the land.'
Archbishop Desmond Tutu, on being awarded the Nobel Prize for Peace

Two books coming out with similar subtitles claim for the Scots the making of the modern world, but the one assumes that the basis was belief in Christian values and the other that it was the search for rational principles. Although they may both see in commerce the vehicle of civilisation, they make a fascinating contrast. There is one further difference between the two books. The second is a serious academic, albeit very readable, study by an American professor of history of the profound influence of a small group of Scottish thinkers, writers and inventors at the end of the Eighteenth Century. The first is also by a professor of history, this time at Oxford University, which is frankly a piece of popularising for a wide readership. The book is quite beautifully illustrated with many full-page colour prints and has been produced in association with a Channel Four series of television programmes.

It has become the practice of university professors of history – a practice not entirely to be decried – to present themselves on television chasing round the countryside, in Niall Ferguson's case the whole world, to bring the past into our view in a fresh and arresting manner. Ferguson has not only a good sense of place, but he and his associates at Channel Four, who initiated the book and the series, have an impeccable sense of timing. In a review of his own book in the *New Statesman* (17.02.03), Ferguson makes it clear that the lesson of his book is for the man he calls 'A Victorian Idealist in the White House'. 'The US', he avers, 'does not stand to gain a great deal from controlling the oilfields of Iraq … No, the culture of imperialism would not be so enduring if it did not have some genuine moral content.' Ferguson writes of President George W. Bush: 'He struck precisely the right, spine-tingling note of righteous vengefulness in his response to 9/11.' That was when Bush called for a 'crusade'. And he praises Blair for the religious fervour of his speech at the 2001 Labour Party Conference, when he spoke of the need to 'reorder this world around us'.. 'bringing democracy and freedom' to the peoples. It might, he says, have been David Livingstone speaking.

A Christian Empire?

Ferguson's thesis is that the British Empire was built by men (very few women) who truly believed that they were helping and enlightening those 'new-caught sullen peoples/ Half devil and half child.' of Kipling's 'Take up the White Man's Burden'. This poem, which is reproduced on the last pages of Ferguson's Empire, was written by Kipling in 1899 in the middle of the disastrous Boer War and was a direct appeal to the United States to shoulder its imperial responsibilities. Of course, it is true that many of Britain's imperialists did genuinely believe in the moral purpose of empire. The Webbs and their fellow members of the *Coefficients* dining club certainly did – after all Beatrice nearly married Joseph Chamberlain. It is much to her credit that she didn't. Commerce, as Ferguson insists, was designed to introduce civilisation with the sanction of Christianity.

Ferguson is quite open about the horrors of the slave trade, about the profits of the opium trade with Hong Kong, about the violence of the colonial wars, about the vicious suppression of the Indian Mutiny, about the massacre at Amritzar, about the bombing of Arab villages, about British racism and all the terrible stories we associate with imperial conquest. If he insists then, as he does, that it was all – or nearly all – done with the best of intentions, it is hard not to add hypocrisy to the list of accusations against imperialism. It is no more acceptable today to ask the people of Iraq to undergo bombardment from Bush, in Ferguson's words, 'because of his faith; not because of "Big Oil" but because of even bigger ideals.' Ferguson happily compares American destruction of the Taliban in Afghanistan and bombing of Belgrade or Baghdad in the name of 'human rights' with the British massacre of the Mahdi dervishes at Omdurman bringing 'justice' to a rogue regime or the Royal Navy's raids on the West African coast as part of the campaign to end the slave trade.

There are two fatal weaknesses in the message that Niall Ferguson has for Messrs Bush and Blair to learn from the history of the British Empire, to combine 'commerce, Christianity and civilisation'. The first is that Ferguson fails to show when conflicts arose between commerce and morality that the latter always prevailed. And I shall have more to say about that. The second is to suppose that the United States has any intention of establishing a world empire in the sense of the rule of freedom and democracy in the countries which it suborns. The world aim of the United States government has been clearly stated by its highest military authorities as 'full spectrum dominance' on land, sea, air and in the stratosphere. The aim of British statesmen in the Nineteenth Century was to bring as much of the world as its widespread navy and quite limited armed strength could encompass within the reach of British trade and investment. The advance of military technology and especially of nuclear weapons, combined with the enormous disparity of wealth between the United States and the rest of the world since the Second World War, has made it possible for the United States to demand of the world's peoples quite simply that they do what its government requires – or else!

After the bombing of Iraq General Tommy Franks may be placed for a time in Baghdad with a major United States military force, but the actual ruling of the country will be left to local bureaucrats and some international presence, whose only requirement will be that they conform to the demands of Washington. That is surely the lesson of previous American involvement in 'peace-keeping' in Bosnia, Kosovo, Afghanistan, or Central Asia. Freedom and democracy will be an optional extra. Of course, much of the British Empire was ruled indirectly, especially, as Ferguson describes, the Princely states of India, but there was an attempt there, as he rightly insists, to establish the rule of law. Ask the Serbs in Kosovo about that. When American military bases are established in Saudi Arabia, Kosovo, Afghanistan or Uzbekistan, President Bush's promise to 'remember our calling as a blessed country to make this world better' and 'confound the designs of evil men' seems soon to be forgotten. There could hardly be on earth a more evil man than President Karimov of Uzbekistan, whose regime has been condemned by Human Rights Watch and one in which the British ambassador has claimed that 'brutality is inherent'.

The assumption of the British imperialists was basically racist – that the coloured peoples were not only hapless infidels, but incapable of ruling themselves or of technological advance without the white man's rule and instruction. To assume this required not only a complete ignorance of history, of the Egyptian, Indian or Chinese civilisations, but a deliberate burying of history in Africa or Latin America and even in India. It is astonishing that Ferguson can write about the Eighteenth Century Indian textile industry without quoting Robert Clive's own description of the wealth of Dacca, comparable to London at the time (now the capital of Bangladesh, today one the poorest countries in the world). Again and again Ferguson underestimates the level of economic development achieved already in the countries which Britain conquered and omits entirely to mention forms of self-government already attained, for example in the Asante Parliament in what is now Ghana. He can even refer to the 'recaptive' slaves in Sierra Leone without discussing their merchants, their schools, universities, hospitals, newspapers, theatres, in the mid-Nineteenth Century, which British colonial rule set out to destroy by the end of the century.

Ferguson's main line of argument about the British Empire is that in fact it was indeed a burden and not a benefit to Britain. It depends what you are referring to as Britain. I have always argued in my books that, after the initial stages of plunder, which established the division between the developed and developing world, the benefits for the British who had to fight the wars and suffer unemployment because of the impoverishment of colonial markets, was very limited. The benefits for the rich were enormous and there was not much 'trickle down' effect. Ferguson sees the great contribution of Britain to the empire in the export of skilled people, amongst whom he numbers several Scottish cousins, and in the export of capital. Both went almost wholly to the United States and to what became the self-governing dominions – Canada, Australia, New Zealand and South Africa. He fails to recognise that most of the United Kingdom's capital accumulation overseas was the result of reinvestment of profits year by year. Keynes once calculated that the gold brought back by Francis Drake to Queen Elizabeth I, reinvested year by year at 5% would just about amount to the value of Britain's foreign investment stock in the 1930s. Nor does Ferguson recognise that much of this stock was the result of switching investment from profits made in India and other colonial territories.

One justification adduced by Ferguson for British colonial rule is that it was not half as bad as that in the other empires – Dutch, Belgian, French, Russian, German, Italian, Japanese. It is a somewhat double-edged compliment. What he is particularly impressed by is the speed with which Britain withdrew from empire. He attributes this to the 'propelling force … of rival empires [German, Japanese, Russian and American] more than indigenous nationalists', although he concedes that the costs of empire, after Britain's financial sacrifices in taking on the German and Japanese at first alone in the Second World War, were increased by 'nationalist insurgency and new military technology'. Ferguson sees the 'symbolic reversal of world history' in the Japanese use of British prisoners to build the Burma railway, when the British had used coolie labour to build their railways all over the world. But he does not ask the obvious question whether this was not the inevitable result of centuries of white men treating other colours as their slaves.

From Colony to Empire

The real historical irony of Britain's loss of empire to the United States – onetime British colony – is not lost on Ferguson. But in asking modern governments of the United States to learn from the British Empire, he is misled. Not only does the colonial origin of the United States of America make empire building anathema, and American superiority in modern technology make it unnecessary, but the religious conviction which Ferguson recognises and approves in President Bush is of a very different nature from that of Queen Victoria's imperialists. Something of the same racism and evangelicalism may be found in both, but the sources are different. British racism until the last 50 years arose from ignorance, from general antipathy to the 'other', to foreigners in general. American racism is based on knowledge, of the very real competition for employment. Similarly, British evangelicalism arose and still arises from an instinct of communal charity towards others, slaves or starving children, sufficiently far away to be no threat. American religion, especially of the 'born again' Christians is intensely personal, concerned with self-improvement and with it the belief that others should be free to do likewise.

One of the central threads in Arthur Herman's brilliant study of the Scottish Enlightenment is the dual source in that remarkable juncture of ideas in Scotland at the end of the Eighteenth Century – the Calvinist belief in God-given personal rectitude and the all embracing rationalism of inquiring minds. This dualism can even be seen in the division of the Scots in the American war of independence between the rebellious Ulster Scots and the loyalist Scots from the Highlands. But the founding fathers combined the two – the frontiersman's belief in the defence of his rights, in the last resort with a gun and the balanced consideration that common sense will prevail – we need only to recite the opening words of the American Declaration of Independence:

> 'We hold these truths to be self-evident, that all men are created equal, that they are endowed by their Creator with certain inalienable rights, that among these are life, liberty and the pursuit of happiness'.

Only the disciples of David Hume and Thomas Reid of Edinburgh could have written those words, and James Madison, Alexander Hamilton and James Wilson were just such disciples.

The result for one-time colonial Americans is that they felt – and still feel – that they were born with a kind of protective personal 'liberty jacket', which they will defend by arms if necessary and which they can sell to the rest of the world. James Madison, agonising over the problem of assuring to such citizens non-oppressive popular rule by a self-governing republic ruling over a country of truly continental scope, had read Hume's 'Idea of a Perfect Commonwealth'. He concluded that the only way to prevent such a republic becoming an empire and therefore acquisitive and corrupt was to balance power between the executive, legislative and judiciary. Virtual gridlock would protect the citizen's liberties. What Madison did not foresee was that private corporate power amounting to what General Eisenhower called a 'military-industrial complex' could begin to finance political parties and determine election results. So it is that today the Executive, the President, can now buy almost absolute power and realise the dreams of the military industrial complex for establishing world power, not by empire, but by 'full spectrum dominance'. Something remains however of the 'liberty belt' in that US citizens can be persuaded that this is what they are exporting to the rest of the world. This is what makes it possible to win support for Bush's provocative stance in threatening war on Iraq. Americans do really feel that they are a 'blessed country'. But Niall Ferguson is wrong to suggest that this provides a moral argument such as Tony Blair is presenting as the excuse for bombing Iraq.

The American Revolution was indeed inspired by the Scottish Enlightenment, and the English rebels – Tom Paine, Shelley, William Godwin and Mary Wolstonecraft – who welcomed the revolution drew their inspiration from the same source, and it had nothing to do with Christianity. Adam Smith, one of the central figures of the Scottish Enlightenment, who is now regarded as the founding father of modern capitalism, condemned empire and far from encouraging the infinite division of labour in large scale commerce, saw in this that 'the minds of men are contracted and rendered incapable of elevation.' Arthur Herman explains at length what some of us have been arguing for a long time, from a careful reading of Smith's *Theory of Moral Sentiments* as well as of his *Wealth of Nations*, that Smith uses his concept of the 'invisible hand' partly in irony, but mostly to emphasise his belief in what he called the 'fellow feeling' of human beings which governed their conduct. America's giant corporations can take no comfort from Adam Smith's morality.

Herman sums up his view of the Scottish Enlightenment in a moving paragraph at the end of his book:

'As the first modern nation and culture, the Scots have by and large made the world a better place. They taught the world that true liberty requires a sense of personal obligation as well as individual rights. They showed that modern life can be spiritually as well as materially fulfilling. They showed how a respect for science and technology can combine with a love for the arts, how private affluence can enhance a sense of civic responsibility, how political and economic democracy can flourish side by side, and how a confidence in the future depends on a reverence for the past. The Scottish mind grasped how, in Hume's words, 'liberty is the perfection of civil society', but 'authority must be acknowledged essential to its very existence'; and how a strong faith in progress also requires a keen appreciation of its limitations.'

Born again Christians may usurp the sentiments and spin the words, but we shall judge them by their deeds.

Michael Barratt Brown

Mapping the Megapower

William Blum, *Rogue State: A Guide to the World's Only Superpower*, Zed Books, 2002, 336 pages, hardback ISBN 1 84277 220 1 £36.95 paperback ISBN 1 84277 221 X £9.99

William Blum tells us that he left the State Department in 1967. He opposed what the United States was doing in Vietnam. Since then he has chronicled the nefarious actions of the World's Only Megapower in many corners of the globe.

First published in 2000, this new and updated edition of *Rogue State* will interest all students of Full Spectrum Dominance. Not because Blum elaborates official US military doctrine, although Full Spectrum Dominance is mentioned in connection with the militarisation of space, but because he paints an extraordinary canvas which sets the context for the emergence of such grotesque aspirations.

Blum's broad themes are encapsulated in his book's three main sections: 'Love/Hate Relationships with Terrorists and Human-Rights Violators'; 'United States Use of Weapons of Mass Destruction'; 'A Rogue State versus the World'. All three are immediately relevant to our present dilemma. To these has been added an introductory essay on 9/11 and the bombing of Afghanistan.

Rogue State is a basic work of reference for the peace movement world-wide. It is written in an engaging manner by a long-time and well-informed dissident.

Tony Simpson

Whose Clangers?

Naomi Klein, *Fences and Windows,* **Flamingo, paperback ISBN 0007150474 £8.99**

Naomi Klein, who established her name with her best seller, *No Logo,* has collected some of her recent articles and speeches under this heading, implying both the obstacles and the opportunities facing the World Social Forum. Martin Wolf of the *Financial Times* has greeted this new book in the pages of *Prospect* (February 2003, p.73) under the title of 'Klein's Clangers', with what I am sure he believes to be a quite devastating put-down – 'arrogant, paranoid, wrong', 'immature', 'hard to tolerate', 'no analysis worthy of the name', 'ancient chestnuts', 'spoiled children of the West' are just some of the insults he hurls at her, in deriding her supposed 'clangers'. Something must have got under his skin.

Wolf decries Klein's critique of the present workings of capitalism, and especially of the World Trade Organisation, World Bank, International Monetary Fund, multinational companies, and pharmaceutical companies as 'a messy mix of populism, anarchism and utopian socialism'. He assumes that this critique means that the protesters at Seattle onwards see no other alternatives than those of Fidel Castro and Subcomandante Marcos, who would scrap all markets and replace representative democracy with mass meetings. By contrast, Wolf believes that 'capitalism [is] the most successful economic system in history; that abandoning markets and profitability, as he assumes Soviet Communism did, delivered only 'tyranny and poverty', that far from democracy being in a bad way he quotes United Nations Development Programme figures to show that in the last 15 years the number of democracies in the world has jumped from 44 to 82, that it is only in underdeveloped economies with mass illiteracy that you find 'demagogy, clientelism and corruption', in strong contrast to the experience in the advanced economies.

What Martin Wolf thinks about the corruption at Enron and other giant US companies, about the withholding of AIDS drugs by the pharmaceutical companies, about the open purchase of votes in the United Nations Security Council by the United States government for its war with Iraq, about the increasing poverty and inequality in large parts of the capitalist world including the advanced economies, about the widespread destruction of the environment by uncontrolled capitalist exploitation, he does not tell us. It is true that the world-wide movement of protest at these outrages has not yet led to the formulation of clear alternatives. But the fact that the capitalist system has had great successes in the past tells us nothing about what human societies will need in the future.

Michael Barratt Brown

Iraq Under Siege New Edition

The Deadly Impact of Sanctions and War

Edited by Anthony Arnove
Preface by Denis Halliday

This new, fully updated edition features essays from world-renowned thinkers including **Noam Chomsky, John Pilger, Howard Zinn, Robert Fisk and Edward Said**. United in their opposition to sanctions and war against Iraq, they outline the suffering that the people of Iraq face, and they explain the implicit dangers of new military action. Written with passion and authority, this unique book will be of interest to anyone who is appalled by the prospect of another war.

"Here is a brilliantly collated body of unrelenting, undeniable evidence of the horrors that the U.S government sanctions are visiting upon the people, in particular the children, of Iraq." **Arundhati Roy**

"This is a very important book and I hope it will be widely read." **Tony Benn, in the *New Statesman***

"This remarkable book is an invaluable documentation of the tragedy in Iraq, and deserves reading by every citizen interested in the appalling reality of US and UK foreign policy." **Edward W. Said**

Published by Pluto Press • January 2003 • Pb • £12.99 • 0 7453 2033 3

Independent Progressive Publishing
www.plutobooks.com

THE FIRE BRIGADES UNION

Bradley House, 68 Coombe Road,
Kingston upon Thames, Surrey, KT2 7AE
Telephone 020 8541 1765
www.fbu.org.uk

We oppose war as a solution to the suffering of the Iraqi people.

We hope for peace and progress in 2003.

The Fire Brigades Union says *"NO"* to war; rather *"INVEST IN PEACE"*

ANDY GILCHRIST – General Secretary
RUTH WINTERS – President